Modern Programming Made Easy

Using Java, Scala, Groovy, and JavaScript

Adam L. Davis

Apress®

Modern Programming Made Easy: Using Java, Scala, Groovy, and JavaScript

Adam L. Davis
Oviedo, Florida
USA

ISBN-13 (pbk): 978-1-4842-2489-2   ISBN-13 (electronic): 978-1-4842-2490-8
DOI 10.1007/978-1-4842-2490-8

Library of Congress Control Number: 2016961534

Managing Director: Welmoed Spahr
Lead Editor: Steve Anglin
Technical Reviewer: Tri Phan
Editorial Board: Steve Anglin, Pramila Balan, Laura Berendson, Aaron Black, Louise Corrigan, Jonathan Gennick, Robert Hutchinson, Celestin Suresh John, Nikhil Karkal, James Markham, Susan McDermott, Matthew Moodie, Natalie Pao, Gwenan Spearing
Coordinating Editor: Mark Powers
Copy Editor: Michael G. Laraque
Compositor: SPi Global
Indexer: SPi Global
Artist: SPi Global

Distributed to the book trade worldwide by Springer Science+Business Media New York, 233 Spring Street, 6th Floor, New York, NY 10013. Phone 1-800-SPRINGER, fax (201) 348-4505, e-mail orders-ny@springer-sbm.com, or visit www.springeronline.com. Apress Media, LLC is a California LLC and the sole member (owner) is Springer Science+Business Media Finance Inc (SSBM Finance Inc). SSBM Finance Inc is a Delaware corporation.

For information on translations, please e-mail rights@apress.com, or visit www.apress.com.

Apress and friends of ED books may be purchased in bulk for academic, corporate, or promotional use. eBook versions and licenses are also available for most titles. For more information, reference our Special Bulk Sales–eBook Licensing web page at www.apress.com/bulk-sales.

Any source code or other supplementary materials referenced by the author in this text are available to readers at www.apress.com. For detailed information about how to locate your book's source code, go to www.apress.com/source-code/. Readers can also access source code at SpringerLink in the Supplementary Material section for each chapter.

Printed on acid-free paper

Dedicated to all teachers, especially those who influenced me.
Thank you for teaching!

Contents at a Glance

Contents

About the Author

Adam L. Davis makes software. He's spent many years developing in Java (since Java 1.2) and has enjoyed using Spring and Hibernate. Since 2006 he's been using Groovy and Grails in addition to Java to create SaaS web applications that help track finances for large institutions (among other things). Adam has a Masters and a Bachelors degree in Computer Science from Georgia Tech. He is also the author of *Learning Groovy* (Apress, 2016).

About the Technical Reviewer

Tri Phan is the founder of the Programming Learning Channel on YouTube. He has more than seven years of experience in the software industry. Specifically, he has worked in many outsourcing companies and written many applications of many fields in different programming languages, such as PHP, Java, and C#. In addition, he has more than six years' experience teaching at international and technological centers, such as Aptech, NIIT, and Kent College.

PART I

■ ■ ■

Starting Out

As computers become more involved in everything we do in society, there will be an ever greater need for people who know how to tell these computers what to do. We call these people many different names: developer, coder, and programmer, among others.

Over the past few decades, a lot has changed in programming. We're going to ignore all that and just get down to the business of programming. If you'd like to learn more about the history of programming, by all means, get a history book from the library.

Figure 1. *Babbage's analytic engine (courtesy of* http://ds.haverford.edu/ bitbybit/*)*

CHAPTER 1

Introduction

In my experience, learning how to program (in typical computer science classes) can be very difficult. The curriculum tends to be boring, abstract, and unattached to "real world" coding. Owing to how fast technology progresses, computer science classes tend to teach material that is very quickly out of date and out of touch. I believe that teaching programming could be much simpler, and I hope this book achieves that goal.

Note There's going to be a lot of tongue-in-cheek humor throughout this book, but this first part is serious. Don't worry, it gets better.

1.1 Problem Solving

Before you learn to program, the task can seem rather daunting, much like looking at a redwood tree on the cover of a book before you climb it. However, over time, you will realize that programming is really about problem-solving.

On your journey toward learning to code, as with so much in life, you will encounter many obstacles. You may have heard it before, but it really is true: the path to success is to try, try, and try again. People who persevere the most tend to be the most successful people.

Programming is fraught with trial and error. Although things will get easier over time, you'll never be right all the time. So, much as with most things in life, you must be patient, diligent, and curious, to be successful.

1.2 About This Book

This book is organized into several chapters, beginning with the most basic concepts. If you already understand a concept, you can safely move ahead to the next chapter. Although this book concentrates on Java, it also refers to other languages, such as Groovy, Scala, and JavaScript, so you will gain a deeper understanding of concepts common to all programming languages.

© Adam L. Davis 2016
A. L. Davis, *Modern Programming Made Easy*, DOI 10.1007/978-1-4842-2490-8_1

Tips   Text styed like this provides additional information that you may find helpful.

 Info   Text styled this way usually refers the curious reader to additional information.

 Warnings   Text such as this cautions the wary reader. Many have fallen along the path of computer programming.

Exercises   This is an exercise. You shouldn't see too many of these.

CHAPTER 2

Software to Install

Before you begin to program, you must install some basic tools.

2.1 Java/Groovy

For Java and Groovy, you will have to install the following:

- JDK (Java Development Kit), such as JDK 8
- IDE (Integrated Development Environment), such as NetBeans 8
- Groovy: A dynamic language similar to Java that runs on the JVM (Java Virtual Machine)

 **Install Java and NetBeans 8**   Download and install the Java JDK 8 with NetBeans.[1] Open NetBeans and select File ➤ New Project... ➤ Java Application

---

 **Install Groovy**   Go and install Groovy[2].

2.1.1 Trying It Out

After installing Groovy, you should use it to try coding. Open a command prompt, type groovyConsole, and hit Enter to begin.

 In groovyConsole, type the following and then hit Ctrl+r to run the code.

1 print "hello"

---

[1]www.oracle.com/technetwork/java/javase/downloads/index.html.
[2]http://groovy.codehaus.org/.

© Adam L. Davis 2016
A. L. Davis, *Modern Programming Made Easy*, DOI 10.1007/978-1-4842-2490-8_2

Because most Java code is valid Groovy code, you should keep the Groovy console open and use it to try out all of the examples from this book.

You can also easily try out Scala and JavaScript in the following ways:

- For JavaScript (JS), just open your web browser and go to jsfiddle.net.[3]

- For Scala, type "scala" in your command prompt or terminal.

2.2 Others

Once you have the preceding installed, you should eventually install the following:

- Scala[4]: An object-oriented language built on the JVM

- Git[5]: A version control program

- Maven[6]: A modular build tool

Go ahead and install these, if you're in the mood. I'll wait.

2.3 Code on GitHub

A lot of the code from this book is available on github.com/modernprog.[7] You can go there at any time, to follow along with the book.

---

[3]http://jsfiddle.net/.
[4]www.scala-lang.org/.
[5]http://git-scm.com/.
[6]https://maven.apache.org/.
[7]https://github.com/modernprog.

CHAPTER 3

The Basics

In this chapter, I'll cover the basic syntax of Java and similar languages.

3.1 Coding Terms

Source file refers to human-readable code. *Binary file* refers to computer-readable code (the compiled code).

In Java, the source files end with .java, and binary files end with .class (also called class files). You *compile* source files using a *compiler*, which gives you binary files.

In Java, the compiler is called javac; in Groovy it is groovyc; and it is scalac in Scala. (See a trend here?)

However, some languages, such as JavaScript, don't have to be compiled. These are called *interpreted languages*.

3.2 Primitives and Reference

Primitive types in Java refer to different ways to store numbers and have historical but also practical significance, for example:

- char: A single character, such as A (the letter *A*)

- byte: A number from -128 to 127 (8 bits[1]). Typically, a way to store or transmit raw data

- short: A 16-bit signed integer. It has a maximum of about 32,000.

- int: A 32-bit signed integer. Its maximum is about 2 to the 31st power.

- long: A 64-bit signed integer. Maximum of 2 to the 63rd power

- float: A 32-bit floating point number. This is an imprecise value that is used for things such as simulations.

---

[1]A bit is the smallest possible amount of information. It corresponds to a 1 or 0.

© Adam L. Davis 2016
A. L. Davis, *Modern Programming Made Easy*, DOI 10.1007/978-1-4842-2490-8_3

- double: Like float but with 64-bit

- boolean: Has only two possible values: true and false (much like 1 bit)

 See Java Tutorial—Data Types[2] for more information.

GROOVY, SCALA, AND JAVASCRIPT

Groovy types are much the same as Java's. In Scala, everything is an object, so primitives don't exist. However, they are replaced with corresponding *value types* (Int, Long, etc.). JavaScript has only one type of number, Number, which is similar to Java's float.

Every other type of variable in Java is a *reference*. It points to some object in memory. You can think of this as an address.

3.3 Strings/Declarations

A *string* is a list of characters (text). It is a very useful built-in class in Java (and most languages). To define a string, you simply surround some text in quotes. For example:

```
1   String hello = "Hello World!";
```

Here the variable hello is assigned the string "Hello World!".

In Java, you must put the type of the variable in the declaration. That's why the first word above is String.

In Groovy and JavaScript, strings can also be surrounded by single quotes ('hello'). Also, declaring variables is different in each language. Groovy allows you to use the keyword def, while JavaScript and Scala use var. For example:

```
1   def hello = "Hello Groovy!" //groovy
2   var hello = "Hello Scala/JS!" //Scala or JS
```

---

²http://docs.oracle.com/javase/tutorial/java/nutsandbolts/datatypes.html.

3.4 Statements

Every statement in Java must end in a semicolon (;). In many other languages, such as Scala, Groovy, and JavaScript, the semicolon is optional, but in Java, it is necessary. Much as how periods at the end of each sentence help you to understand the written word, the semicolon helps the compiler understand the code.

By convention, we usually put each statement on its own line, but this is not required, as long as semicolons are used to separate each statement.

3.5 Assignment

Assignment is an extremely important concept to understand, but it can be difficult for beginners. However, once you understand it, you will forget how hard it was to learn.

Let's start with a metaphor. Imagine you want to hide something valuable, such as a gold coin. You put it in a safe place and write the address on a piece of paper. This paper is like a reference to the gold. You can pass it around and even make copies of it, but the gold remains in the same place and does not get copied. On the other hand, anyone with the reference to the gold can get to it. This is how a *reference variable* works.

Let's look at an example.

```
1   String gold = "Au";
2   String a = gold;
3   String b = a;
4   b = "Br";
```

After running the preceding code, gold and a refer to the string "Au", while b refers to "Br".

3.6 Class and Object

A *class* is the basic building block of code in object-oriented languages. A class typically defines state and behavior. The following class is named SmallClass:

```
1   package com.example.mpme;
2   public class SmallClass {
3   }
```

Class names always begin in an uppercase letter in Java. It's common practice to use CamelCase to construct the names. This means that instead of using spaces (or anything else) to separate words, we uppercase the first letter of each word.

The first line is the package of the class. A package is like a directory on the file system. In fact, in Java, the package must actually match the path to the Java source file. So, the preceding class would be located in the path com/example/mpme/ in the source file system.

An *object* is an instance of a class in memory. Because a class can have multiple values within it, an instance of a class will store those values.

Create a Class

- Open your IDE (NetBeans).

- Right-click your Java project and choose New ➤ Java Class.

3.6.1 Properties and Methods

Next you might want to add some properties and methods to your class. A *property* is a value associated with a particular object. A *method* is a block of code on a class.

```
1   package com.example.mpme;
2   public class SmallClass {
3       String name;
4       String getName() {return name;}
5       void print() {System.out.println(name);}
6   }
```

In the preceding code, name is a property and getName and print are methods.

3.6.2 Groovy Classes

Groovy is extremely similar to Java but always defaults to public.

```
1   package com.example.mpme;
2   class SmallClass {
3       String name //property
4       def print() { println(name) } //method
5   }
```

Groovy also automatically gives you "getter" and "setter" methods for properties, so writing the getName method would have been redundant.

3.6.3 JavaScript Prototypes

Although JavaScript has objects, it doesn't have a class keyword. Instead, it uses a concept called prototype. For example, creating a class looks like the following:

```
1   function SmallClass() {}
2   SmallClass.prototype.name = "name"
3   SmallClass.prototype.print = function() { print(this.name) }
```

Here name is a property and print is a method.

3.6.4   Scala Classes

Scala has a very concise syntax, which puts the properties of a class in parentheses. For example:

```
1    class SmallClass(var name:String) {
2        def  print = println(name)
3    }
```

3.6.5   Creating a New Object

In all four languages, creating a new object uses the new keyword. For example:

```
1    sc = new  SmallClass();
```

3.7   Comments

As a human, it is sometimes useful for you to leave notes in your source code for other humans—and even for yourself, later. We call these notes *comments*. You write comments thus:

```
1    String gold = "Au"; // this is a comment
2    String a = gold; // a is now "Au"
3    String b = a; // b is now  "Au"
4    b = "Br";
5    /* b is now "Br".
6       this is still a comment */
```

Those last two lines demonstrate multiline comments. So, in summary,

- Two forward slashes denote the start of a single-line comment.
- Slash-asterisk marks the beginning of a multiline comment.
- Asterisk-slash marks the end of a multiline comment.

Comments are the same in all languages covered in this book.

3.8   Summary

In this chapter, you learned the basic concepts of programming.

- Compiling source files into binary files
- How objects are instances of classes
- Primitive types, references, and strings
- Variable assignment
- How source code comments work

PART II

■ ■ ■

Glorified Calculator

Math is the most basic operation a computer can perform. In fact, in the early days of computers, it was the only thing they could do. A computer was basically a glorified calculator. So, it makes sense then that one of the first things a programmer learns is math.

However, unlike most books, this one is going to teach using interesting concepts. Instead of employing abstract or boring concepts, I'm going to talk about zombies, vampires, and various other lethal monsters.

Figure 1. *Dragon*

CHAPTER 4

Math

(Or *Maths*, if you prefer.)

4.1   Adding, Subtracting, Etc.

Your friend Bob was just bitten by a zombie but escaped alive. Unfortunately, there is now one more zombie to worry about.

```
1    zombies = zombies + 1;
```

There's a shorter way to write the same thing (and we are pressed for time here; the zombies are coming).

```
1    zombies += 1;
```

Actually, there's an even shorter way to write this, and it's call the *increment operator.*

```
1    zombies++;
```

Luckily, there's also a *decrement operator* (to use when we kill a zombie).

```
1    zombie--;
```

Adding and subtracting are easy enough, but what about their cousins, multiplying and dividing? Luckily these symbols are the same in virtually every programming language: * and /.

```
1    int legs = zombies * 2;
2    int halfZombies = zombies / 2;
```

Numbers written in Java are of type int by default. But what if we want to deal with fractions (such as one-third)?

```
1    float oneThirdZombies = zombies / 3.0f;
```

No, 3.0f is not a typo. The f makes 3 a float. You can use lower- or uppercase letters (D means double; F means float; and L means long).

This is where math starts to get tricky. To engage *float division* (remember, float is an imprecise number), we need 3 to be a float. If we instead wrote zombies / 3, this would result in *integer division*, and the remainder would be lost. For example, 33 / 3 is 10.

MODULO

You don't really need to understand Modulo, but if you want to, keep reading. Imagine that you and three buddies want to attack a group of zombies. You have to know how many each of you has to kill, so that each of you kills an equal number of zombies. For this you do integer division.

```
1   int numberToKill = zombies / 4;
```

But you want to know how many will be left over. For this, you require *modulo* (%):

```
1   int leftOverZombies = zombies % 4;
```

This gives you the *remainder* of dividing zombies by four.

4.2 More Complex Math

If you want to do anything other than add, subtract, multiply, divide, and modulo, you will have to use the java.util.Math class.

Let's say you want to raise a number to the power of 2. For example, if you want to estimate the exponentially increasing number of zombies, as follows:

```
1   double nextYearEstimate = Math.pow(numberOfZombies, 2.0d);
```

This type of method is called a *static method*. (Don't worry, you'll learn more about this later.) Here's a summary of the most commonly used methods in java.util.Math.

- abs: Returns the absolute value of a value

- min: The minimum of two numbers

- max: The maximum of two numbers

- pow: Returns the value of the first argument raised to the power of the second argument

- sqrt: Returns the correctly rounded positive square root of a double value

- cos: Returns the trigonometric cosine of an angle

- sin: Returns the trigonometric sine of an angle

- tan: Returns the trigonometric tangent of an angle

 For a list of all the methods in Math, see the Java docs.[1]

Sine   If you're unfamiliar with sine and cosine, they are very useful whenever you want to draw a circle, for example. If you're on your computer right now, and want to learn more about sine and cosine, please look at this animation[2] referenced in the footnote at the end of this page and keep watching it until you understand the sine wave.

4.3   Random Numbers

The easiest way to create a random number is to use the Math.random() method.

The random() method returns a double value greater than or equal to zero and less than one.

For example, to simulate a roll of the dice (to determine who gets to deal with the next wave of zombies), use the following:

```
1   int roll = (int) (Math.random() * 6);
```

This would result in a random number from 0 to 5.

JavaScript also has a Math.random() method. For example, to get a random integer between min (included) and max (excluded) you would do the following:

```
1   Math.floor(Math.random() * (max - min)) + min;
```

However, if you want to create lots of random numbers in Java, it's better to use the java.util.Random class instead. It has several different methods for creating random numbers, including:

- nextInt(int n): A random number from 0 to n (not including n).

- nextInt(): A random number uniformly distributed across all possible int values

- nextLong(): Same as nextInt() but for long

- nextFloat(): Same as nextInt() but for float

---

[1]http://docs.oracle.com/javase/6/docs/api/java/lang/Math.html.
[2]https://upload.wikimedia.org/wikipedia/commons/0/08/Sine_curve_drawing_animation.gif.

- nextDouble(): Same as nextInt() but for double

- nextBoolean(): True or false

- nextBytes(byte[] bytes): Fills the given byte array with r
andom bytes

You must first create a new Random object, then you can use it to create random numbers, as follows:

```
1    Random randy = new Random();
2    int roll6 = randy.nextInt(6) + 1; // 1 to 6
3    int roll12 = randy.nextInt(12) + 1; // 1 to 12
```

Now you can create random numbers and do math with them. Hurray!

Q **Seeds** If you create a Random with a seed (e.g., new Random(1234)), it will always generate the same sequence of random numbers when given the same seed.

4.4   Summary

In this chapter, you learned how to program math, such as:

- How to add, subtract, multiply, divide, and modulo

- Use the Math library in Java

- Create random numbers

CHAPTER 5

Arrays, Lists, Sets, and Maps

So far, I've only talked about single values, but in programming, you often have to work with large collections of values. For this, we have many data structures that are built into the language. These are similar for Java, Groovy, Scala, and even JavaScript.

5.1 Arrays

An *array* is a fixed size collection of data values. Honestly, you probably won't use an array very often, but it's an important concept to learn.

You declare an array-type in Java by appending [ ] to the type. For example, an array of ints is defined as int[ ].

```
1   int[] vampireAges = new int[10]; // ten vampires
```

Accessing the values in an array uses the same square-bracket syntax, such as

```
1   vampireAges[0] = 1565; // first vampire
```

As you can see, the first index of an array is zero. Things tend to start at zero when programming; try to remember this.

Patient 0   Here's a helpful metaphor: the first person to start an outbreak (a zombie outbreak, for example) is known as patient zero, not patient one. Patient one is the *second* person infected.

This also means that the *last* index of the array is always one less than the size of the array. This is also true for lists.

```
1   vampireAges[9] = 442; // last vampire
```

You can reassign and access array values just like any other variable.

© Adam L. Davis 2016
A. L. Davis, *Modern Programming Made Easy*, DOI 10.1007/978-1-4842-2490-8_5

```
1   int year = 2016; // current year?
2   int firstVampBornYear = year - vampireAges[0];
```

You can also declare arrays of objects as well. In this case, each element of the array is a reference to an object in memory.

```
1   Vampire[] vampires = new Vampire[10]; // Vampire array with length 10
```

You can also populate your array directly, such as if you're creating an array of strings, for example.

```
1   String[] names = {"Dracula", "Edward"};
```

Unfortunately, arrays are difficult to use in Groovy and the Array object in JavaScript is more like a Java List. Java arrays are a somewhat low-level structure, used only for performance reasons.

5.2 Lists

Of course, we don't always know how many elements we need to store in an array. For this reason (and many others), programmers invented List, a resizable collection of ordered elements.

In Java, you create List in the following way:

```
1   List<Vampire> vampires = new  ArrayList<>();
```

The angle-brackets (<>) define the *generic type* of the list—what can go into the list. You can now add vampires to this list all day, and it will expand, as necessary, in the background.

You add to List like this:

```
1   vampires.add(new  Vampire("Count Dracula", 1897));
```

List also contains tons of other useful methods, including:

- size(): Gets the size of List

- get(int index): Gets the value at that index

- remove(int index): Removes the value at that index

- remove(Object o): Removes the given object

- isEmpty(): Returns true only if List is empty

- clear(): Removes all values from List

🔑 In Java, List has many different implementations, but we'll just focus on two (don't worry about the details here).

- java.util.ArrayList
- java.util.LinkedList

The only difference you should care about is that, in general, LinkedList grows faster, while ArrayList's get() method is faster.

You'll learn how to loop through lists, arrays, and sets (and what "loop" means) in the next chapter. For now, just know that lists are a fundamental concept in programming.

5.2.1   Groovy Lists

Groovy has a simpler syntax for creating lists, which is built into the language.

```
1   def list = []
2   list.add(new Vampire("Count Dracula", 1897))
3   // or
4   list << new Vampire("Count Dracula", 1897)
```

5.2.2   Scala Lists

In Scala, you create a list and add to a list in a slightly different way:

```
1   var list = List[Vampire]();
2   list :+ new Vampire("Count Dracula", 1897)
```

Also, this actually creates a new list, instead of modifying the existing list. This is because the default List in Scala is *immutable,* meaning it cannot be modified. Although this may seem strange in conjunction with *functional* programming, it makes parallel programming (programming for multiple processors) easier.

5.2.3   JavaScript Arrays

As mentioned earlier, JavaScript uses Array[1] instead of List.

---

[1] https://developer.mozilla.org/en-US/docs/Web/JavaScript/Reference/Global_Objects/Array.

Arrays can be created much like lists in Groovy. However, the methods available are somewhat different. For example, push is used instead of add.

```
1   def array = []
2   array.push(new Vampire("Count Dracula", 1897))
```

You can also declare the initial values of Array. For example, the following two lines are equivalent:

```
1   def years = [1666, 1680, 1722]
2   def years = new Array(1666, 1680, 1722)
```

To add to the confusion, arrays in JavaScript can be accessed much like Java arrays. For example:

```
1   def firstYear = years[0]
2   def size = years.length
```

5.3   Sets

Set is much like List, but each value or object can only have one instance in Set.

Set has many of the same methods as List. In particular, it is missing the methods that use an index, because Set is not necessarily in any particular order.

```
1   Set<String> dragons = new HashSet<>();
2   dragons.add("Lambton");
3   dragons.add("Deerhurst");
4   dragons.size(); // 2
5   dragons.remove("Lambton");
6   dragons.size(); // 1
```

In Java, there is such a thing as SortedSet, which is implemented by TreeSet. For example, let's say you wanted a sorted list of names, as follows:

```
1   SortedSet<String> dragons = new TreeSet<>();
2   dragons.add("Lambton");
3   dragons.add("Smaug");
4   dragons.add("Deerhurst");
5   dragons.add("Norbert");
6   System.out.println(dragons);
7   // [Deerhurst, Lambton, Norbert, Smaug]
```

TreeSet will magically always be sorted in the proper order.

🔑 Okay, it's not really magic. The object to be sorted must implement the *comparable* interface, but you haven't learned about interfaces yet.

JavaScript does not yet have a built-in Set class.

5.4 Maps

Map is a collection of keys associated with values. It may be easier to understand with an example.

```
1   Map<String,String> map = new HashMap<>();
2   map.put("Smaug", "deadly");
3   map.put("Norbert", "cute");
4   map.size(); // 2
5   map.get("Smaug"); // deadly
```

Map also has the following methods:

- containsKey(Object key): Returns true, if this map contains a mapping for the specified key

- containsValue(Object value): Returns true, if this map maps one or more keys to the specified value

- keySet(): Returns a Set view of the keys contained in this map

- putAll(Map m): Copies all of the mappings from the specified map to this map

- remove(Object key): Removes the mapping for a key from this map, if it is present

5.4.1 Groovy Maps

Just as for List, Groovy has a simpler syntax for creating and editing Map.

```
1   def map = ["Smaug": "deadly"]
2   map.Norbert = "cute"
3   println(map) // [Smaug:deadly, Norbert:cute]
```

5.4.2 Scala Maps

Scala's Map syntax is also somewhat shorter.

```
1   var map = Map("Smaug" -> "deadly")
```

```
2  var map2 = map + ("Norbert" -> "cute")
3  println(map2) // Map(Smaug -> deadly, Norbert -> cute)
```

As with List, Scala's default Map is also immutable.

5.4.3   JavaScript Maps

JavaScript does not yet have a built-in Map class, but it can be approximated by using the built-in Object[2] syntax. For example:

```
1  def map = {"Smaug": "deadly", "Norbert": "cute"}
```

You could then use either of the following to access map values: map.Smaug or map["Smaug"].

5.5   Summary

This chapter introduced you to the following concepts:

- *Arrays*: Primitive collections of data

- *Lists*: An expandable collection of objects or values

- *Sets*: A collection of unique objects or values

- *Maps*: A dictionary-like collection

---

[2]https://developer.mozilla.org/en-US/docs/Web/JavaScript/Reference/Global_Objects/Object.

CHAPTER 6

Conditionals and Loops

To rise above the label of *calculator*, a programming language must have conditional statements and loops.

A *conditional statement* is a statement that may or may not execute, depending on the circumstances.

A *loop* is a statement that gets repeated multiple times.

6.1 If, Then, Else

The most basic conditional statement is the *if* statement. It is the same in all languages covered in this book. For example:

```
1    if (vampire) { // vampire is a boolean
2            useWoodenStake();
3    }
```

Curly brackets ({}) define a block of code (in Java, Scala, Groovy, and JavaScript). To define what should happen if your condition is false, you use the else keyword.

```
1    if (vampire) {
2            useWoodenStake();
3    } else {
4            useAxe();
5    }
```

Actually, this can be shortened, because we only have one statement per condition.

```
1    if (vampire) useWoodenStake();
2    else useAxe();
```

But it's generally better to use the curly-bracket style in Java. If you have multiple conditions you have to test for, you can use the else if style, such as the following:

```
1    if (vampire) useWoodenStake();
2    else if (zombie) useBat();
3    else useAxe();
```

© Adam L. Davis 2016
A. L. Davis, *Modern Programming Made Easy*, DOI 10.1007/978-1-4842-2490-8_6

6.2   switch Statements

Sometimes you have so many conditions that your else if statements span several pages. In this case, you might consider using the switch keyword. It allows you to test for several different values of the same variable. For example:

```
1   switch (monsterType) {
2   case "Vampire": useWoodenStake(); break;
3   case "Zombie": useBat(); break;
4   case "Orc": shoutInsult();
5   default: useAxe();
6   }
```

The case keyword denotes the value to be matched.

The break keyword always causes the program to exit the current code block. This is necessary in a switch statement; otherwise, every statement after the case will be executed. For example, when monsterType is "Orc", shoutInsult and useAxe are executed.

The default keyword denotes the code to execute if none of the cases is matched. It is much like the final else block of an if/else block.

There is more to switch statements, but this involves concepts I'll cover later on, so we'll return to this topic.

6.3   Boolean Logic

Figure 6-1. *Formal Logic—XKCD 1033 (courtesy http://xkcd.com/1033/)*

Computers use a special kind of math called *Boolean logic* (it's also called *Boolean algebra*). All you really need to know are the following three Boolean operators and six comparators:

&&—AND: True only if left and right values are `true`.

||—OR y if either left or right value is `true`.

!—NOT: Negates a Boolean (`true` becomes `false`; `false` becomes `true`.

==: Equals

!=: Does not equal

<: Less than

>: Greater than

<=: Less than or equal

>=: Greater than or equal

Conditions (such as `if`) operate on Boolean values (`true`/`false`)—the same boolean type that you learned about in Chapter 3. When used properly, all the preceding operators result in a Boolean value.

For example:

```
1  if (age > 120 && skin == Pale && !winkled) {
2          probablyVampire();
3  }
```

6.4 Looping

The two simplest ways to loop are the `while` loop and `do`/`while` loop.

The `while` loop simply repeats until the *loop condition* becomes `false`.

```
1  boolean repeat = true;
2  while (repeat) {
3          doSomething();
4          repeat = false;
5  }
```

The preceding would call the `doSomething()` method once. The loop condition in the preceding code is `repeat`. This is a simple example. Usually, the loop condition would be something more complex.

The do loop is like the `while` loop, except that it always goes through at least one time. For example:

```
1  boolean repeat = false;
2  do {
3          doSomething();
4  } while(repeat);
```

It's often helpful to increment a number in your loop, for example:

```
1   int i = 0;
2   while (i < 10) {
3           doSomething(i);
4           i++;
5   }
```

The preceding loop can be condensed using the for loop.

```
1   for  (int  i = 0; i < 10; i++) {
2           doSomething(i);
3   }
```

The for loop has an initiation clause, a loop condition, and an increment clause. This style of loop is useful for looping through an array with an index. For example:

```
1   String[] strArray = {"a", "b", "c"};
2   for (int i = 0; i < strArray.length; i++)
3           System.out.print(strArray[i]);
```

This would print "abc." The preceding loop is equivalent to the following:

```
1   int i = 0;
2   while  (i < strArray.length) {
3       String str = strArray[i];
4           System.out.print(str);
5           i++;
6   }
```

In Java, you can write for loops in a more concise way for an array or collection (list or set). For example:

```
1   String[] strArray = {"a", "b", "c"};
2   for  (String str : strArray)
3               System.out.print(str);
```

This is called a for each loop. Note that it uses a colon instead of a semicolon.

6.5 Summary

In this chapter, you learned about the following:

- Using the if statement
- How to use Boolean logic
- switch statements
- Using for, do, and while loops

CHAPTER 7

Methods

A *method* is a series of statements combined into one block inside a class and given a name. In the Cold War days, these were called sub-routines, and many other languages call them *functions*. However, the main difference between a method and a function is that a method has to be associated with a class, whereas a function does not.

7.1 Call Me

Methods exist to be called. You can think of a method as a message that is sent or a command given. To *call* a method (also known as *invoking* a method), you simply write the name of the object, a dot, then the method name. For example:

```
1  Dragon dragon = new Dragon();
2  dragon.fly(); // dragon is the object, and fly is the method
```

The fly method would be defined within the Dragon class.

```
1  public void fly() {
2          // flying code
3  }
```

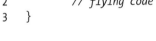 **Void**   In Java, void means that no result is returned.

Methods can also have parameters. A *parameter* is a value (or reference value) that is part of a method call. Together, the method's name and parameters are called the *method signature*. For example, the following method has two parameters:

```
1  public void fly(int x, int y) {
2          // fly to that x, y coordinate.
3  }
```

© Adam L. Davis 2016
A. L. Davis, *Modern Programming Made Easy*, DOI 10.1007/978-1-4842-2490-8_7

7.1.1   Non-Java

Other languages define methods (or functions) differently. For example, in Groovy, you can use the def keyword to define a method (in addition to Java's normal syntax), as follows:

```
1   def fly() { println("flying") }
```

Scala also uses the def keyword to define a method, but you also need an equal (=) sign.

```
1   def fly() = { println("flying") }
```

JavaScript uses the function keyword to define a function:

```
1   function fly() { alert("flying") }
```

7.2   Break It Down

Methods also exist to organize your code. One rule of thumb is to never have a method that is longer than one screen. It makes no difference to the computer, but it makes all the difference to humans (including you).

It's also very important to name your method well. For example, a method that fires an arrow should be called "fireArrow," and not "fire," "arrow," or "arrowFartBigNow."

This may seem like a simple concept, but you might be surprised by how many people fail to grasp it.

7.3   Return to Sender

Often, you will want a method to return a result. In Java, you use the return keyword to do this. For example:

```
1   public Dragon makeDragonNamed(String name) {
2   return new Dragon(name);
3   }
```

Once the return statement is reached, the method is complete. Whatever code called the method will resume execution.

In some languages, such as Groovy and Scala, the return keyword is optional. Whatever value is put on the last line will get returned. For example (Groovy):

```
1   def makeDragonNamed(name) {
2           new Dragon(name)
3   }
```

7.4   Static

In Java, a *static method* is a method that is not linked to an object instance. However, it must be part of a class.

For example, the random() method in the java.util.Math class we learned about earlier is a static method.

To declare a static method, you simply add the word static, as in the following:

```
1   public static String makeThemFight(Dragon d, Vampire v) {
2              // a bunch of code goes here.
3   }
```

Because Java is an object-oriented programming language (OOP), in theory, static methods should be used sparingly, because they are not linked to any object. However, in real life, you will see them *a lot.*

7.5   Varargs

Varargs, or "variable arguments," allow you to declare a method's last parameter with an ellipsis (. . .), and it will be interpreted to accept any number of parameters (including zero) and convert them into an array in your method. For example, see the following code:

```
1   void printSpaced(Object... objects) {
2           for (Object o : objects) System.out.print(o + " ");
3   }
```

Putting it all together, you can have the following code (with output in comments):

```
1   printSpaced("A", "B", "C"); // A B C
2   printSpaced(1, 2, 3); // 1 2 3
```

7.6   Main Method

Now that you know about static methods, you can finally run a Java program (sorry it took so long). Here's how you create an executable *main method* in Java:

```
1   import static java.lang.System.out;
2   /** Main class. */
3   public class Main {
4       public static void main(String ... args) {
5           out.println("Hello World!");
6       }
7   }
```

Then, to compile it, open your command prompt or terminal and type the following:

```
1   javac Main.java
2   java Main
```

Or, in NetBeans, do the following:

- Right-click the Main class.

- Choose Run File.

7.7 Exercises

✏ **Try out methods**   After you've created the Main class, try adding some methods to it. Try calling methods from other methods and see what happens.

✏ **Lists, Sets, and Maps**   In Java, all of these data structures are under the java.util package. So, start by importing this whole package:

```
1   import    java.util.*;
```

Then go back to Chapter 5 and try out some of the code there.

7.8 Summary

This chapter explained the concept of methods and how they should be used.

We also put together everything you've learned up to this point and made a small Java application.

PART III

■ ■ ■

Polymorphic Spree

The title of this part is a play on the name of the band Polyphonic Spree.[1]

The term *polymorphism* refers to a principle in biology according to which an organism or species can have many different forms or stages. This principle can also be applied to object-oriented programming (OOP) languages such as Java. Subclasses of a class can define their own unique behaviors and yet share some of the same functionality of the parent class.

Figure 1. *Mythical creatures (clockwise from bottom-left): unicorn, griffon, phoenix, dragon, roc (center)*

[1]www.thepolyphonicspree.com/.

CHAPTER 8

Inheritance

Inheritance is a good way to share functionality between objects. When a class has a parent class, we say it *inherits* the fields and methods of its parent.

In Java, you use the extends keyword to define the parent of a class. For example:

```
1   public class Griffon extends FlyingCreature {
2   }
```

Another way to share functionality is called *composition*. This means that an object holds a reference to another object and uses it to do things. For example:

```
1   class Griffon {
2       Wing leftWing = new Wing()
3       Wing rightWing = new Wing()
4       def fly() {
5           leftWing.flap()
6           rightWing.flap()
7       }
8   }
```

This way, you can also have a Bird class that also uses the Wing class, for example.

8.1   Objectify

What is an object anyway? An *object* is an instance of a class (in Java, Groovy, and Scala).

In Java, classes have constructors, which can have multiple parameters for initializing the object. For example, see the following:

```
1   class   FlyingCreature   {
2           String name;
3           // constructor
4           public   FlyingCreature(String name) {
5               this.name = name;
6           }
7   }
```

The constructor of FlyingCreature has one parameter, name, which is stored in the name field. A constructor must be called using the new keyword, to create an object, for example:

```
1   String name = "Bob";
2   FlyingCreature fc = new  FlyingCreature(name);
```

Once an object is created, it can be passed around (this is called a *pass by reference*). Although String is a special class, it is a class, so you can pass around an instance of it, as shown in the preceding code.

8.1.1   JavaScript

In JavaScript, a constructor is a function used to define a prototype. Inside the constructor, the prototype is referred to using the this keyword. For example, you could define a Creature in JavaScript, as follows:

```
1   function Creature(n) {
2       this.name = n;
3   }
4   var  bob = new  Creature('Bob');
```

▓ **Note**   All functions and objects in JavaScript have a prototype.

8.2   Parenting 101

A *parent class* defines shared functionality (methods) and state (fields) that are common to multiple classes.

For example, let's create a FlyingCreature class that defines a fly() method and has a name.

```
1    class FlyingCreature {
2            String name;
3            public FlyingCreature(String name) {
4                    this.name = name;
5            }
6            public void fly() {
7                    System.out.println(name + " is flying");
8            }
9    }
10   class Griffon extends FlyingCreature {
11           public  Griffon(String n) { super(n); }
12   }
13   class Dragon extends FlyingCreature {
```

```
14          public  Dragon(String n) { super(n); }
15  }
16  public  class  Parenting  {
17          public static void main(String ... args) {
18                  Dragon d = new  Dragon("Smaug");
19                  Griffon g = new   Griffon("Gilda");
20                  d.fly(); // Smaug is flying
21                  g.fly(); // Gilda is flying
22          }
23  }
```

There are two classes in the preceding code, Griffon and Dragon, that extend FlyingCreature. FlyingCreature is sometimes referred to as the *base class*. Griffon and Dragon are referred to as *subclasses*.

Keep in mind that you can use the parent class's type to refer to any subclass. For example, you can make any flying creature fly, as follows:

```
1   FlyingCreature creature = new Dragon("Smaug");
2   creature.fly(); // Smaug is flying
```

This concept is called *extension*. You *extend* the parent class (FlyingCreature, in this case).

8.2.1   JavaScript

In JavaScript, we can use prototypes to extend functionality.

For example, let's say we have a prototype called Undead.

```
1   function Undead() {
2       this.dead = false;
3       this.living = false;
4   }
```

Now let's create two other constructors, Zombie and Vampire.

```
1   function Zombie() {
2       Undead.call(this);
3       this.deseased = true;
4       this.talk = function() { alert("BRAINS!") }
5   }
6   Zombie.prototype = Object.create(Undead.prototype);
7
8   function Vampire() {
9       Undead.call(this);
10       this.pale = true;
11       this.talk = function() { alert("BLOOD!") }
12   }
13   Vampire.prototype = Object.create(Undead.prototype);
```

Note how we set Zombie's and Vampire's prototype to an instance of the Undead prototype. This allows zombies and vampires to inherit the properties of Undead, while having different talk functions, as follows:

```
1   var zombie = new Zombie();
2   var vamp = new Vampire();
3   zombie.talk();   //BRAINS
4   zombie.deseased;  // true
5   vamp.talk();     //BLOOD
6   vamp.pale; //true
7   vamp.dead; //false
```

8.3   Packages

In Java (and related languages, Groovy, and Scala), a *package* is a namespace for classes. *Namespace* is a just shorthand for a bin of names. Every modern programming language has some type of namespace feature. This is necessary, owing to the nature of having lots and lots of classes in typical projects.

As you learned in Chapter 3, the first line of a Java file defines the package of the class, for example:

```
1   package com.github.modernprog;
```

Also, there is a common understanding that a package name corresponds to a URL (github.com/modernprog, in this case). However, this is not necessary.

8.4   Public Parts

You might be wondering why the word *public* shows up everywhere in the examples so far. The reason has to do with encapsulation. *Encapsulation* is a big word that just means "a class should expose as little as possible to get the job done" (some things are meant to be private). This helps reduce complexity of code and, therefore, makes it easier to understand and think about.

There are three different keywords in Java for varying levels of "exposure."

- Private: Only this class can see it.

- Protected: Only this class and its descendants can see it.

- Public: Everyone can see it.

There's also "default" protection (absent of a keyword), which limits use to any class in the same package.

This is why classes tend to be declared `public`, because, otherwise, their usage would be very limited. However, a class can be private, for example, when declaring a class within another class, as follows:

```
1   public class Griffon extends FlyingCreature {
2           private class GriffonWing {}
3   }
```

8.4.1   JavaScript

JavaScript does not have the concept of packages, but, instead, you must rely on `scope`. Variables are only visible inside the function they were created in, except for *global* variables.

8.5   Interfaces

An *interface* declares method signatures that will be implemented by classes that extend the interface. This allows Java code to work on several different classes without necessarily knowing what specific class is "underneath" the interface.

For example, you could have an interface with one method, as follows:

```
1   public interface  Beast  {
2           int getNumberOfLegs(); // all interface methods are public
3   }
```

Then you could have several different classes that *implement* that interface.

```
1   public class Griffon extends FlyingCreature implements  Beast {
2           public int getNumberOfLegs() { return 2; }
3   }
4   public class Unicorn implements Beast {
5           public int getNumberOfLegs() { return 4; }
6   }
```

▒ **Note**   JavaScript does not have an equivalent concept to interface.

8.6   Abstract Class

An *abstract* is a class that can have abstract methods but cannot have instances. It is something like an interface with functionality, however, a class can only extend one superclass, while it can implement multiple interfaces.

For example, to implement the preceding Beast interface as an abstract class, you can do the following:

```
1  public abstract class Beast {
2          public abstract int getNumberOfLegs();
3  }
```

Then you could add non-abstract methods and/or fields.

8.7 Enums

In Java, the enum keyword creates a type-safe, ordered list of values. For example:

```
1  public enum BloodType {
2          A, B, AB, O, VAMPIRE, UNICORN;
3  }
```

An enum variable can only point to one of the values in the enum. For example:

```
1  BloodType type = BloodType.A;
```

The enum is automatically given a bunch of methods, such as

- values(): Gives you an array of all possible values in the enum (static)

- valueOf(String): Converts the given string into the enum value with the given name

- name(): An instance method on the enum that gives its name

Also, enums have special treatment in switch statements. For example, in Java, you can use an abbreviated syntax (assuming type is a BloodType).

```
1  switch (type) {
2          case VAMPIRE: return vampire();
3          case UNICORN: return unicorn();
4          default: return human();
5  }
```

8.8 Annotations

Java annotations allow you to add meta-information to Java code that can be used by the compiler, various APIs, or even your own code at runtime.

The most common annotation you will see is the @Override annotation, which declares to the compiler that you are overriding a method. For example:

```
1   @Override
2   public String toString() {
3           return "my own string";
4   }
```

This is useful, because it will cause a compile-time error if you mistype the method name, for example.

Other useful annotations are those in javax.annotation, such as @Nonnull and @Nonnegative, which declare your intentions.

Annotations such as @Autowired and @Inject are used by direct-injection frameworks such as Spring and Google Guice,[1] repectively, to reduce "wiring" code.

8.9   Autoboxing

Although Java is an object-oriented language, this sometimes conflicts with its primitive types (int, long, float, double, etc.). For this reason, Java added autoboxing and unboxing to the language.

8.9.1   Autoboxing

The Java compiler will automatically wrap a primitive type in the corresponding object when it's necessary, for example, when passing in parameters to a function or assigning a variable, as in the following: Integer number = 1.

8.9.2   Unboxing

This is simply the reverse of autoboxing. The Java compiler will unwrap an object to the corresponding primitive type, when possible. For example, the following code would work: double d = new Double(1.1) + new Double(2.2).

8.10   Summary

After reading this chapter, you should understand OOP, polymorphism, and the definitions of the following:

- Extension and composition
- Public vs. private vs. protected
- Class, abstract class, interface, enum
- Annotations
- Autoboxing and unboxing

---

[1] http://code.google.com/p/google-guice/.

CHAPTER 9

Design Patterns

In object-oriented programming (OOP), design patterns are useful organizations of state and behavior that make your code more readable, testable, and extensible.

9.1 Observer

The *observer* pattern allows you to broadcast information from one class to many others, without them having to know about each other directly.

It is often used with events. For example, the KeyListener, MouseListener, and many other "Listener" interfaces in Java Swing implement the observer pattern and use events.

Another example of this pattern is the Observable class and Observer interfaces supplied in Java. Here is a simple example that simply repeats the same event forever:

```
1   import       java.util.Observable;
2
3   public class EventSource extends Observable implements Runnable {
4       @Override
5       public void run() {
6           while (true) {
7               notifyObservers("event");
8           }
9       }
10  }
```

Although the event is simply a string in this example, it could be of any type.

The following class implements the Observer interface and prints out any events of type String:

```
1   import java.util.Observable;
2   import java.util.Observer;     /* this is Event Handler */
3
```

© Adam L. Davis 2016
A. L. Davis, *Modern Programming Made Easy*, DOI 10.1007/978-1-4842-2490-8_9

```
4    public class StringObserver implements Observer {
5        public void update(Observable obj, Object event) {
6            if (event instanceof String) {
7                System.out.println("\nReceived Response: " + event );
8            }
9        }
10   }
```

To run this example, simply do the following:

```
1    final EventSource eventSource = new EventSource();
2    // create an observer
3    final StringObserver stringObserver = new StringObserver();
4    // subscribe the observer to the event source
5    eventSource.addObserver(stringObserver);
6    // starts the event thread
7    Thread thread = new  Thread(eventSource);
8    thread.start();
```

9.2 MVC

Model–view–controller (MVC) is possibly the most popular software design pattern (Figure 9-1). As the name suggests, it consists of three major parts:

- *Model*: The data or information being shown and manipulated

- *View*: What actually defines how the model is shown to the user

- *Controller*: Defines how actions can manipulate the model

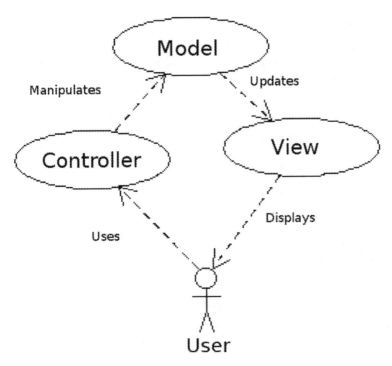

Figure 9-1. *Model–view–controller*

This design allows the controller, model, and view to know very little about each other. This reduces *coupling*—the degree to which different components of the software rely on other components. When you have low coupling, your software is easier to understand and easier to extend.

We will look at a great example of MVC when I talk about grails.

9.3 DSL

A *domain specific language* (DSL) is a custom programming language made for a specific domain. For example, you can think of HTML as a DSL for displaying web pages.

Some languages allow you such freedom that you can create a DSL inside the language. For example, Groovy and Scala allow you to override the math symbols (+, -, etc.). The other freedoms of these languages (optional parentheses and semicolons) allow for DSL-like interfaces. We call these DSL-like interfaces *fluent interfaces*.

You can also create fluent interfaces in Java and other languages.

9.3.1 Closures

Within Groovy, you can take a block of code (a closure) as a parameter and then call it, using a local variable as a delegate. For example, imagine that you have the following code for sending SMS texts:

```
1    class SMS {
2            def from(String fromNumber) {
3                    // set the from
4            }
5            def to(String toNumber) {
6                    // set the to
7            }
8            def body(String body) {
9                    // set the body of text
10           }
11           def send() {
12                   // send the text.
13           }
14   }
```

In Java, you'd have to use this the following way:

```
1    SMS m = new  SMS();
2    m.from("555-432-1234");
3    m.to("555-678-4321");
4    m.body("Hey there!");
5    m.send();
```

In Groovy, you can add the following static method to the SMS class for DSL-like usage:

```
1    def static send(block) {
2            SMS m = new SMS()
3            block.delegate = m
4            block()
5            m.send()
6    }
```

This sets the SMS object as a delegate for the block, so that methods are forwarded to it. With this you can now do the following:

```
1    SMS.send {
2            from '555-432-1234'
3            to '555-678-4321'
4            body 'Hey there!'
6    }
```

9.3.2   Overriding Operators

In Scala or Groovy, you could create a DSL for calculating speeds with specific units, such as meters per second.

```
1   val time =  20 seconds
2   val dist =  155 meters
3   val speed =  dist / time
4   println(speed.value) //  7.75
```

By overriding operators, you can constrain users of your DSL to reduce errors. For example, time/dist would cause a compilation error in this DSL.

Here's how you would define this DSL in Scala:

```
1   class Second(val value: Float) {}
2   class MeterPerSecond(val  value:  Float) {}
3   class Meter(val value: Float) {
4     def /(sec: Second) = {
5       new MeterPerSecond(value / sec.value)
6     }
7   }
8   class EnhancedFloat(value: Float) {
9     def seconds = {
10      new   Second(value)
11    }
12    def  meters = {
13      new  Meter(value)
14    }
15  }
16  implicit  def  enhanceFloat(f:  Float) =  new  EnhancedFloat(f)
```

Q Scala has the implicit keyword, which allows the compiler to do implicit conversions for you.

Notice how the divide / operator is defined just like any other method.

---

i In Groovy, you overload operators by defining methods with special names[1] such as plus, minus, multiply, div, etc.

---

[1] http://groovy.codehaus.org/Operator+Overloading.

9.4 Actors

The *actor design pattern* is a useful pattern for developing concurrent software. In this pattern, each actor executes in its own thread and manipulates its own data. The data cannot be manipulated by anyone else. Messages are passed between actors to cause them to change data (Figure 9-2).

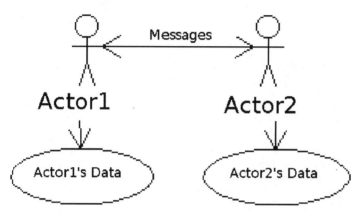

Figure 9-2. *Actors*

▦ **Note** When data can only be changed by one thread at a time, we call it *thread-safe*.

There are many implementations of this pattern that you can use, including the following:

- Akka[2]
- Jetlang[3]
- FunctionalJava[4]
- GPars[5]

---

[2]http://akka.io/.
[3]https://code.google.com/p/jetlang/.
[4]http://functionaljava.org/.
[5]http://gpars.codehaus.org/.

CHAPTER 10

Functional Programming

Functional programming (FP) is a programming style that focuses on functions and minimizes changes of state (using immutable data structures). It is closer to expressing solutions mathematically, rather than through step-by-step instructions.

In FP, functions should be "side-effect free" (nothing outside the function is changed) and *referentially transparent* (a function returns the same value every time when given the same arguments).

FP is an alternative to the more common *imperative programming*, which is closer to telling the computer the steps to follow.

Although functional-programming could be achieved in Java pre-Java-8,[1] Java 8 enabled language-level FP support with lambda expressions and *functional interfaces*.

Java 8, JavaScript, Groovy, and Scala all support functional-style programming, although they are not FP languages.

■ **Note**   Prominent functional programming languages such as Common Lisp, Scheme, Clojure, Racket, Erlang, OCaml, Haskell, and F# have been used in industrial and commercial applications by a wide variety of organizations. Clojure[2] is a Lisp-like language that runs on the JVM.

10.1   Functions and Closures

Of course, "functions as a first-class feature" is the basis of functional programming. *First-class feature* means that a function can be used anywhere a value can be used.

For example, in JavaScript, you can assign a function to a variable and call it

```
1   var func = function(x) { return x + 1; }
2   var three = func(2); //3
```

---

[1] http://functionaljava.org/.
[2] http://clojure.org/.

© Adam L. Davis 2016

A. L. Davis, *Modern Programming Made Easy*, DOI 10.1007/978-1-4842-2490-8_10

Although Groovy doesn't have first-class functions, it has something very similar: closures. A closure is simply a block of code wrapped in curly brackets with parameters defined left of the -> (arrow). For example:

```
1    def closr = {x -> x + 1}
2    println( closr(2) ); //3
```

If a closure has one argument, it can be referenced as it in Groovy. For example:

```
1    def closr = {it + 1}
```

Java 8 introduced the lambda expression, which is something like a closure that implements an interface. The main syntax of a lambda expression is "parameters -> body." The Java compiler uses the context of the expression to determine which functional interface is being used (and the types of the parameters). For example:

```
1    Function<Integer,Integer> func = x -> x + 1;
2    int three = func.apply(2);
```

Here, the functional interface is Function, which has the apply method. The return value and parameter type of both Integers, thus Integer, Integer, are the generic type parameters.

Q In Java 8, a *functional interface* is defined as an interface with exactly one abstract method. This even applies to interfaces that were created with previous versions of Java.

In Scala, everything is an expression, and functions are a first-class feature. Here's a function example in Scala:

```
1    var f = (x: Int) => x + 1;
2    println(f(2));
```

Although both Java and Scala are statically typed, Scala actually uses the right-hand side to infer the type of function being declared, whereas Java does the opposite.

Q In Java, Groovy, and Scala, the return keyword can be omitted, if there is one expression in the function/closure. However, in Groovy and Scala, the return keyword can also be omitted, if the returned value is the last expression.

10.2   Map/Filter/etc.

Once you have mastered functions, you quickly realize that you need a way to perform operations on collections (or sequences or streams) of data.

Because these are common operations, *sequence operations,* such as map, filter, reduce, etc., were invented.

We'll use JavaScript for the examples in this section, because it is easier to read, and the function names are fairly standard across programming languages.

map translates or changes input elements into something else (Figure 10-1).

```
1    var names = persons.map(function(person) { return person.name })
```

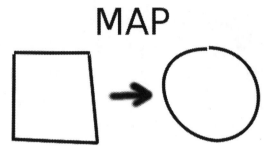

Figure 10-1. *Map*

filter gives you a subset of elements (what returns true from some *predicate* function [Figure 10-2]).

```
1    var adults = persons.filter(function(person) { return person.age >= 18 })
```

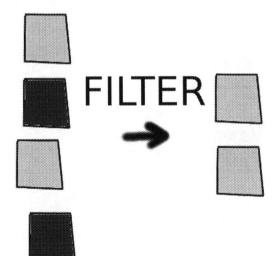

Figure 10-2. *Filter*

reduce performs a reduction on the elements (Figure 10-3).

```
1   var totalAge = persons.reduce(function(total, p) { return total+p.age }, 0)
```

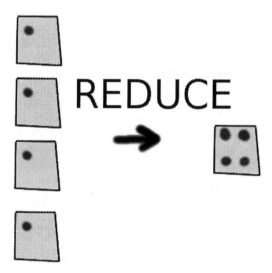

Figure 10-3. *Reduce*

limit gives you only the first N elements (Figure 10-4).

Figure 10-4. *Limit*

concat combines two different collections of elements (Figure 10-5).

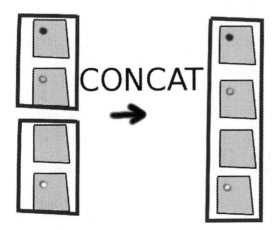

Figure 10-5. *Concat*

10.3   Immutability

Immutability and FP go together like peanut butter and jelly. Although it's not necessary, they blend nicely.

In purely functional languages, the idea is that each function has no effect outside itself—no side effects. This means that every time you call a function, it returns the same value given the same inputs.

To accommodate this behavior, there are *immutable* data-structures. An immutable data-structure cannot be directly changed but returns a new data-structure with every operation.

For example, as you learned earlier, Scala's default Map is immutable.

```
1   val map = Map("Smaug" -> "deadly")
2   val map2 = map + ("Norbert" -> "cute")
3   println(map2) // Map(Smaug -> deadly, Norbert -> cute)
```

So, in the preceding, map would remain unchanged.

Each language has a keyword for defining immutable variables (values).

- Scala uses the val keyword to denote immutable values, as opposed to var, which is used for mutable variables.

- Java has the final keyword for declaring immutable variables.

- In addition to the final keyword, Groovy includes the @Immutable annotation[3] for declaring a whole class immutable.

- JavaScript uses the const keyword.[4]

---

[3]http://groovy.codehaus.org/Immutable+AST+Macro.
[4]https://developer.mozilla.org/en-US/docs/Web/JavaScript/Guide/Values,_
variables,_and_literals#Constants.

For example (in Groovy):

```
1   public class Centaur {
2       final String name
3       public Centaur(name) {this.name=name}
4   }
5   Centaur c = new Centaur("Bane");
6   println(c.name) // Bane
7
8   c.name = "Firenze" //error
```

This works for simple references and primitives, such as numbers and strings, but for things such as lists and maps, it's more complicated. For these cases, open source immutable libraries have been developed for the languages in which it's not included, such as the following:

- Guava[5] for Java and Groovy

- Immutable-JS[6] for JavaScript

10.4   Java 8

In Java 8, the *Stream* interface was introduced. A stream is like an improved iterator that supports chaining methods to perform complex operations.

To use a stream, you must first create one in one of the following ways:

- Collection's stream() *method or* parallelStream() *method*: These create a stream backed by the collection.

- Arrays.stream() *method*: Used for converting arrays to streams

- Stream.generate(Supplier<T> s): Returns an infinite sequential stream in which each element is generated by the given supplier

- Stream.iterate(T seed, UnaryOperator<T> f): Returns an infinite sequential ordered stream produced by iterative application of a function to an initial element seed, producing a stream consisting of seed, f(seed), f(f(seed)), etc.

Once you have a stream, you can then use filter, map, and reduce operations to concisely perform calculations on the data. For example:

```
1   String longestName = dragons.stream()
2       .filter(d -> d.name != null)
3       .map(d -> d.name)
4       .reduce((n1, n2) -> n1.length() > n2.length() ? n1 : n2)
5       .get();
```

---

[5]https://code.google.com/p/guava-libraries/.
[6]https://github.com/facebook/immutable-js.

10.5 Groovy

In Groovy, findAll and other methods are available on every object but are especially useful for lists and sets. The following method names are used in Groovy:

- findAll: Much like filter, it finds all elements that match a closure.

- collect: Much like map, this is an iterator that builds a collection.

- inject: Much like reduce, it loops through the values and returns a single value.

- each: Iterates through the values using the given closure

- eachWithIndex: Iterates through with two parameters: a value and an index

- find: Finds the first element that matches a closure

- findIndexOf: Finds the first element that matches a closure and returns its index

- any: True if any element returns true for the closure

- every: True if all elements return true for the closure

For example, the following assumes dragons is a list of dragon objects:

```
1   String longestName = dragons.
2   findAll { it.name != null }.
3   collect { it.name }.
4   inject("") { n1, n2 -> n1.length() > n2.length() ? n1 : n2 }
```

 Remember that it in Groovy can be used to reference the single argument of a closure.

10.6 Scala

Scala has many such methods on its built-in collections, including the following:

- map: Converts values

- flatMap: Converts values and then concatenates the results together

- filter: Limits the returned values, based on some Boolean expression

- find: Returns the first value matching the given predicate

- forAll: True only if all elements match the given predicate
- exists: True if at least one element matches the given predicate
- foldLeft: Reduces the values to one value using the given closure, starting at the last element and going left
- foldRight: Same as foldLeft, but starting from the first value and going up

For example, you can use map to perform an operation on a list of values, as follows:

```
1   val list = List(1, 2, 3)
2   list.map(_ * 2) // List(2, 4, 6)
```

Q Much like it in Groovy, in Scala, you can use the underscore to reference a single argument.

Assuming dragons is a List of dragon objects, you can do the following in Scala:

```
1   var longestName = dragons.filter(_ != null).map(_.name).foldRight("")(
2       (n1:String,n2:String) => if (n1.length() > n2.length()) n1 else n2)
```

10.7 Summary

In this chapter, you should have learned about

- Functions as a first-class feature
- Map/Filter/Reduce
- Immutability and how it relates to FP
- Various features supporting FPs in Java, Groovy, Scala, and JavaScript

CHAPTER 11

Refactoring

Refactoring[1] means changing code in a way that has no effect on functionality. It is only meant to make the code easier to understand or to prepare for some future addition of functionality For example, sometimes you refactor code to make it easier to test.

There are two categories of refactoring I am going to cover, Object-Oriented and Functional, corresponding to the two different programming styles.

11.1 Object-Oriented Refactoring

The following actions are common refactorings in OOP:

- Changing a method or class name (renaming)
- Moving a method from one class to another (delegation)
- Moving a field from one class to another
- Creating a new class using a set of methods and fields from a class
- Changing a local variable to a class field
- Replacing a bunch of literals (strings or numbers) with a constant (static final)
- Moving a class from an anonymous class to a top level class
- Renaming a field

11.2 Functional Refactoring

The following actions are common refactorings in FP:

- Renaming a function
- Wrapping a function in another function and calling it

---

[1]Yes *refactoring* is a word!

© Adam L. Davis 2016
A. L. Davis, *Modern Programming Made Easy*, DOI 10.1007/978-1-4842-2490-8_11

- Inline a function wherever it is called

- Extract common code into a function (the opposite of the previous.

- Renaming a function parameter

- Adding a parameter

You might notice some similarities between both lists. The principles of refactoring are universal.

11.3   Refactoring Examples

Here are some examples of refactoring code:

11.3.1   Renaming a Method

Before:

```
1   public static void main(String...args) {
2       animateDead();
3   }
4   public  static void  animateDead() {}
```

After:

```
1   public static void main(String...args) {
2       doCoolThing();
3   }
4   public  static void  doCoolThing() {}
```

11.3.2   Moving a Method from One Class to Another (Delegation)

Before:

```
1   public static void main(String...args) {
2       animateDead();
3   }
4   public  static void  animateDead() {}
```

After:

```
1   public class Animator() {
2       public void animateDead() {}
3   }
4   public static void main(String...args) {
5       new Animator().animateDead();
6   }
```

11.3.3 Replacing a Bunch of Literals (Strings or Numbers) with a Constant (Static Final)

Before:

```
1   public static void main(String...args) {
2       animateDead(123);
3       System.out.println(123);
4   }
5   public static void animateDead(int n) {}
```

After:

```
1   public static final int NUM = 123;
2   public static void main(String...args) {
3       animateDead(NUM);
4       System.out.println(NUM);
5   }
6   public static void animateDead(int n) {}
```

11.3.4 Renaming a Function

Before:

```
1   function castaNastySpell() { /* cast a spell here */ }
```

After:

```
1   function castSpell() { /* cast a  spell here  */ }
```

11.3.5 Wrapping a Function in Another Function and Calling It

Before:

```
1   castSpell('my cool spell');
```

After:

```
1   (function(spell) { castSpell(spell) })('my cool spell');
```

11.3.6   Inline a Function Wherever It Is Called

Before:

```
1   function castSpell(spell) { alert('You cast ' + spell); }
2   castSpell('crucio');
3   castSpell('expelliarmus');
```

After:

```
1   alert('You cast ' + 'crucio');
2   alert('You cast ' + 'expelliarmus');
```

11.3.7   Extract Common Code into a Function (the Opposite of the Previous)

Before:

```
1   alert('You cast crucio');
2   alert('You cast expelliarmus');
```

After:

```
1   function castSpell(spell) { alert('You cast ' + spell); }
2   castSpell('crucio');
3   castSpell('expelliarmus');
```

CHAPTER 12

■ ■ ■

Utilities

The java.util package contains many useful classes for everyday programming. Likewise, JavaScript and other languages come with many built-in objects for doing common tasks. I am going to cover a few of these.

12.1 Dates and Times

You should never store date values as text. It's too easy to mess up.

© Adam L. Davis 2016
A. L. Davis, *Modern Programming Made Easy*, DOI 10.1007/978-1-4842-2490-8_12

12.1.1   Java 8 Date-Time

Java 8 comes with a new and improved Date-Time application program interface (API) that is much safer, easier to read, and more comprehensive than the previous API.

For example, creating a date looks like the following:

```
1   LocalDate date = LocalDate.of(2014, Month.MARCH, 2);
```

There's also a `LocalDateTime` class to represent date and time, `LocalTime` to represent only time, and `ZonedDateTime` to represent a time with a time zone.

Before Java 8, there were only two built-in classes to help with dates: `Date` and `Calendar`. These should be avoided.

- `Date` actually represents both a date and time.

- `Calendar` is used to manipulate dates.

In Java 7, you'd have to do the following to add five days to a date:

```
1   Calendar cal = Calendar.getInstance();
2   cal.setTime(date);
3   cal.add(5, Calendar.DAY);
```

12.1.2   Groovy Date

Groovy has a bunch of built-in features that make dates easier to work with. For example, numbers can be used to add/subtract days, as follows:

```
1   def date = new Date() + 5; //adds 5 days
```

Groovy also has TimeCategory[1] for manipulating dates and times. This lets you add and subtract any arbitrary length of time. For example:

```
1   import groovy.time.TimeCategory
2   now = new Date()
3   println now
4   use(TimeCategory) {
5       nextWeekPlusTenHours = now + 1.week + 10.hours - 30.seconds
6   }
7   println nextWeekPlusTenHours
```

A *Category* is a class that can be used to add functionality to other existing classes. In this case, TimeCategory adds a bunch of methods to the `Integer` class.

---

[1]http://groovy.codehaus.org/api/groovy/time/TimeCategory.html.

CATEGORIES

This is one of the many *meta-programming* techniques available in Groovy. To make a category, you create a bunch of static methods that operate on one parameter of a particular type (e.g., `Integer`). When the category is used, that type appears to have those methods. The object on which the method is called is used as the parameter. Take a look at the documentation for TimeCategory for an example of this in action.

12.1.3   JavaScript Date

JavaScript also has a Date[2] object.

You can create an instance of a Date object in several ways (these all create the same date):

```
1   Date.parse('June 13, 2014')
2   new Date('2014-06-13')
3   new Date(2014, 5, 13)
```

Note that if you adhere to the international standard (yyyy-MM-dd), a UTC time zone will be assumed; otherwise, it will assume you want a local time.

As usual with JavaScript, the browsers all have slightly different rules, so you have to be careful with this.

⚠ **Don't ever use getYear**   In both Java and JavaScript, the Date object's getYear() method doesn't do what you think and should be avoided. For historical reasons, getYear does not actually return the year (e.g., 2014). You should use getFullYear() in JavaScript and LocalDate or LocalDateTime in Java 8.

12.1.4   Java DateFormat

Although DateFormat is in java.text, it goes hand-in-hand with java.util.Date.

The SimpleDateFormat is useful for formatting dates in any format you want. For example:

```
1   SimpleDateFormat sdf = new  SimpleDateFormat("MM/dd/yyyy");
2   Date date = new  Date();
3   System.out.println(sdf.format(date));
```

---

[2]http://mzl.la/1unepot.

This would format a date per the US standard: month/day/year.

 More Formatting   See SimpleDateFormat[3] for more information.

12.2 Currency

In Java, Currency is useful if your code has to deal with currencies in several countries. It provides the following methods:

- getSymbol(): Currency symbol for the default locale

- getSymbol(Locale): Currency symbol for the given locale

- static getAvailableCurrencies(): Returns the set of available currencies.

For example:

```
1   String pound = Currency.getSymbol(Locale.UK);
```

12.3 TimeZone

In Java 8, time zones are represented by the java.time.ZoneId class. There are two types of ZoneIds, fixed offsets and geographical regions. This is to compensate for practices such as daylight saving time, which can be very complex.

You can get an instance of a ZoneId in many ways, including the following two:

```
1   ZoneId mountainTime = ZoneId.of("America/Denver");
2   ZoneId myZone = ZoneId.systemDefault();
```

To print out all available IDs, use getAvailableZoneIds(), as follows:

```
1   System.out.println(ZoneId.getAvailableZoneIds());
```

   Write a program that does this and run it.

---

[3]http://docs.oracle.com/javase/6/docs/api/java/text/SimpleDateFormat.html.

12.4 Scanner

Scanner can be used to parse files or user input. It breaks the input into tokens, using a given pattern, which is whitespace by default ("whitespace" refers to spaces, tabs, or anything that is not visible in text).

For example, use the following to read two numbers from the user:

```
1    System.out.println("Please type two numbers");
2    Scanner sc = new Scanner(System.in);
3    int num1 = sc.nextInt();
4    int num2 = sc.nextInt();
```

 Write a program that does this and try it out.

PART IV

■ ■ ■

Real Life

After you master the basics of programming, you might think you're done. Unfortunately, it's not that easy. In the real world, you have to learn a lot more, if you want to be a real computer wizard.

Figure 1. *Merlin and King Arthur*

CHAPTER 13

Building

The *build process* is one of compiling the source files of a project and producing a finished product.

In some companies, there are whole teams whose sole job is the build process.

There are many other build tools, but I'm just going to cover three:

- Ant[1]
- Maven[2]
- Gradle[3]

13.1 Ant

Ant is the first really popular project builder for Java that existed. It is XML-based and requires you to create tasks in XML that can be executed by Ant.

A *task* is a division of work. Tasks depend on other tasks. For example, the "jar" task usually depends on the "compile" task. Although Maven threw away the task concept, it was used again in Gradle.

Critics of Ant complain that it uses XML (a much-loathed format) and requires a lot of work to do simple things.

13.2 Maven

Maven is an XML-based declarative project manager. Maven is used for building Java projects but is capable of much more. Maven is also a set of standards that allows Java/JVM developers to easily define and integrate dependencies into large projects. Maven somewhat replaces Ant but can also integrate with it and other build tools.

Maven was mostly a reaction to the huge number of open source libraries Java projects tend to rely on. It has a built-in standard for dependency management (managing the interdependencies of open source libraries).

---

[1]http://ant.apache.org/.
[2]http://maven.apache.org/.
[3]www.gradle.org/.

© Adam L. Davis 2016
A. L. Davis, *Modern Programming Made Easy*, DOI 10.1007/978-1-4842-2490-8_13

Although Maven is an Apache open source project, it could be said that the core of Maven is *Maven Central*, a repository of open source libraries run by Sonatype, the company behind Maven. There are many other repositories that follow the Maven standard, such as JFrog's jCenter,[4] so you are not restricted to Maven Central.

Ivy[5] is a similar build tool, but is more closely related to Ant.

Many build tools, such as Ivy and Gradle, build on top of Maven's concept.

13.2.1 Using Maven

The main file that defines a Maven project is the *POM* (Project Object Model). The POM file is written in XML and contains all of the dependencies, plug-ins, properties, and configuration data that is specific to the current project. The POM file is generally composed of the following:

- Basic properties (artifactId, groupId, name, version, packaging)

- Dependencies

- Plug-ins

There is a Maven plug-in for every major Java-based IDE out there (Eclipse, NetBeans, and IntelliJ IDEA), and they are very helpful. You can use the Maven plug-in to create your project, add dependencies, and edit your POM files.

13.2.2 Starting a New Project

There is a simple way to create a new configuration file (pom.xml) and project folders using the archetype:generate command.

```
1   mvn archetype:generate
```

That will list all the different kinds of projects you can create. Pick a number representing the type of project you want (there are 726 options right now), then answer some questions regarding the name of your project. After that process, run the following command to build the project:

```
1   mvn package
```

If you want to use any additional third-party libraries, you will have to edit the POM to include each dependency. Fortunately, most IDEs make it easy to add dependencies to the POM.

---

[4]https://bintray.com/bintray/jcenter.
[5]http://ant.apache.org/ivy/.

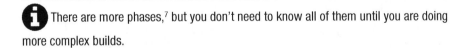

Maven the Complete Reference   Maven the Complete Reference[6] is available online if you want to learn more.

13.2.3   Life Cycle

Maven uses a declarative style (unlike Ant, which uses a more imperative approach). This means that instead of listing the steps to take, you describe what should happen during certain phases of the build. The phases in Maven are as follows:

- `validate`: Validates that the project is correct and all necessary information is available

- `compile`: Compiles the source code of the project

- `test`: Tests the compiled source code, using a suitable unit-testing framework

- `package`: Takes the compiled code and packages it in its distributable format, such as a JAR

- `integration-test`: Processes and deploys the package, if necessary, into an environment in which integration tests can be run

- `verify`: Runs any checks to verify that the package is valid and meets quality criteria

- `install`: Installs the package into the local repository, for use as a dependency in other projects locally

- `deploy`: Copies, in an integration or release environment, the final package to the remote repository, for sharing with other developers and projects

There are more phases,[7] but you don't need to know all of them until you are doing more complex builds.

---

[6]www.sonatype.com/books/mvnref-book/reference/.
[7]https://maven.apache.org/guides/introduction/introduction-to-the-lifecycle.
html#Lifecycle_Reference.

13.2.4   Executing Code

Sometimes, however, you just need more control over your build. In Maven, you can execute Groovy code, Ant build files, Scala code, and you can even write your own plugins in Groovy.

For example, you can put Groovy code in your POM file in the following way:

```
1   <plugin>
2    <groupId>org.codehaus.groovy.maven</groupId>
3    <artifactId>gmaven-plugin</artifactId>
4    <executions>
5     <execution>
6       <id>groovy-magic</id>
7       <phase>prepare-package</phase>
8       <goals>
9         <goal>execute</goal>
10      </goals>
11       <configuration>
12         <source>
13           def depFile = new  File(project.build.outputDirectory,
              'deps.txt')
14
15           project.dependencies.each() {
16             depFile.write("${it.groupId}:${it.artifactId}:${it.
              version}")
17           }
18
19           ant.copy(todir: project.build.outputDirectory ) {
20             fileset(dir: project.build.sourceDirectory)
21           }
22         </source>
23       </configuration>
24     </execution>
25    </executions>
26   </plugin>
```

The preceding code would write out every dependency of the project into the file deps.txt. Then it would copy all of the source files into the project.build. outputDirectory (usually target/classes).

 See Chapters 2, 3, and 4 in *The Maven Cookbook*.[8]

ˢhttp://books.sonatype.com/mcookbook/reference/index.html

13.3 Gradle

Gradle is a Groovy-based DSL (domain specific language) system for building projects. The Gradle web site describes it as follows:

> *Gradle combines the power and flexibility of Ant with the dependency management and conventions of Maven into a more effective way to build. Powered by a Groovy DSL and packed with innovation, Gradle provides a declarative way to describe all kinds of builds through sensible defaults.*
>
> —*gradle.org*[9]

13.3.1 Projects and Tasks

Each Gradle build is composed of one or more projects, and each project is composed of tasks.

The *core* of the Gradle build is the build.gradle file, which is called the *build script*. Tasks are defined by writing task, then a task-name followed by a closure. For example:

```
1   task upper {
2           String someString = 'test'
3           println "Original: $someString"
4           println "Uppercase: " + someString.toUpperCase()
5   }
```

Tasks can contain any Groovy code, but you can take advantage of existing Ant tasks; for example:

```
ant.loadfile(srcFile: file, property: 'x') //loads file into x
ant.checksum(file: file, property: "z") // put checksum into z
println ant.properties["z"] //accesses ant property z
```

The preceding code would load a file into Ant-property "x", save the file's checksum in Ant-property "z", and then print out that checksum.

Much as in Ant, a task can depend on other tasks, which means they must be run before the task. You simply call dependsOn with any number of task names as arguments. For example:

```
1   task buildApp {
2           dependsOn clean, installApp, processAssets
3   }
```

---

[9]www.gradle.org/.

13.3.2   Plug-ins

Gradle core has very little built-in. It has powerful plug-ins to allow it to be very flexible. A plug-in can do one or more of the following:

- Add tasks to the project (e.g., compile, test)

- Pre-configure added tasks with useful defaults

- Add dependency configurations to the project

- Add new properties and methods to existing type, via extensions

We're going to concentrate on building Java-based projects, so we'll be using the java plug-in; however, Gradle is not limited to Java projects!

```
1   apply plugin: 'java'
```

This plug-in uses Maven's conventions. For example, it expects to find your production source code under src/main/java and your test source code under src/test/java.

13.3.3   Maven Dependencies

Every Java project tends to rely on many open source projects to be built. Gradle builds on Maven, so you can easily include your dependencies, using a simple DSL, such as in the following example:

```
1   apply plugin: 'java'
2
3   sourceCompatibility = 1.7
4
5   repositories {
6           mavenLocal()
7           mavenCentral()
8   }
9
10  dependencies {
11          compile 'com.google.guava:guava:14.0.1'
12          compile 'org.bitbucket.dollar:dollar:1.0-beta2'
13          testCompile group: 'junit', name: 'junit', version: '4.+'
14          testCompile "org.mockito:mockito-core:1.9.5"
15  }
```

This build script uses sourceCompatibility to define the Java source code version of 1.7 (which is used during compilation). Next, it tells Maven to use the local repository first (mavenLocal), then Maven Central.

In the dependencies block, this build script defines two dependencies for the compile scope and two for testCompile scope. Jars in the testCompile scope are only used in tests and won't be included in any final products.

The line for JUnit shows the more verbose style for defining dependencies.

ℹ Online Documentation   Gradle has a huge online user guide available online at gradle.org.[10]

---

[10]www.gradle.org/docs/current/userguide/userguide.html.

CHAPTER 14

Testing

Testing is a very important part of software creation. Without automated tests, it's very easy for bugs to creep into software.

In fact, some go as far as to say that you should write tests *before* you write the code. This is called *TDD* (test-driven development).

14.1 Types of Tests

The following are different types of tests you might write:

- *Unit test*: Test conducted on a single API call or some isolated code

- *Integration test*: Test of a higher order code that requires a test harness, mocking, etc.

- *Acceptance test*: High-level test that matches the business requirements

- *Compatibility*: Making sure that things work together

- *Functionality*: Ensuring that stuff works

- *Black box*: Test conducted without knowing/thinking about what's going on in the code

- *White box*: Tests written with the inside of code in mind

- *Gray box*: Hybrid of black and white box testing

- *Regression*: Creating a test after finding a bug, to ensure that the bug does not reappear

- *Smoke*: A huge sampling of data

- *Load/Stress/Performance*: How the system handles load

The type and number of tests you write vary, based on a number of factors. The simpler a piece of code is, the less testing it requires. For example, a "getter" or "setter" does not require a test at all.

© Adam L. Davis 2016
A. L. Davis, *Modern Programming Made Easy*, DOI 10.1007/978-1-4842-2490-8_14

14.2   JUnit

JUnit[1] is a simple framework to write repeatable tests.

A typical JUnit 4.x test consists of multiple methods annotated with the @Test annotation.

At the top of every JUnit test class, you should include all the static Assert methods, and annotations, like so:

```
1   import static org.junit.Assert.*;
2   import org.junit.Test;
3   import org.junit.Before;
4   import org.junit.After;
```

Use @Before, to annotate initialization methods that are run before every test, and @After, to annotate breakdown methods that are run after every test.

Each test method should test one thing, and the method name should reflect the purpose of the test. For example:

```
1   @Test
2   public void toStringYieldsTheStringRepresentation() {
3           String[] array = {"a", "b", "c"};
4           ArrayWrapper<String> arrayWrapper = new
            ArrayWrapper<String>(array);
5           assertEquals("[a, b, c]", arrayWrapper.toString());
6   }
```

14.2.1   Hamcrest

In more recent versions (JUnit 4.4+[2]), JUnit also includes Hamcrest matchers.

```
1   import static org.hamcrest.Matchers.*;
2   import static org.junit.Assert.*;
```

You can create more readable tests using the Hamcrest core matchers. For example:

```
1   @Test
2   public void sizeIs10() {
3           assertThat(wrapper.size(), is(10));
4   }
```

---

[1]http://junit.org/.
[2]http://junit.sourceforge.net/doc/ReleaseNotes4.4.html.

14.2.2   Assumptions

Often, there are variables outside of a test that are beyond your control but which your test assumes to be true. When an assumption fails, it shouldn't necessarily mean that your test fails. For this purpose, JUnit added assumeThat, which you may import, like so:

```
1    import static org.junit.Assume.*;
```

You can verify assumptions before your assertions in your tests. For example:

```
1    assumeThat(File.separatorChar, is('/'));
```

When an assumption fails, the test is either marked as passing or ignored, depending on the version of JUnit.[3]

---

[3]http://junit.sourceforge.net/doc/ReleaseNotes4.4.html.

CHAPTER 15

Input/Output

15.1 Files

In Java, the java.io.File class is used to represent files and directories. For example:

```
1   File file = new  File("path/file.txt");
2   File dir = new File("path/"); //directory
```

Java 7 added several new classes and interfaces for manipulating files and filesystems. This new application program interface (API) allows developers to access many low-level OS operations that were not available from the Java API before, such as the WatchService and the ability to create links (in Linux/Unix operating systems).

Paths are used to more consistently represent file or directory paths.

```
1   Path path = Paths.get("/path/file");
```

This is shorthand for the following:

```
1   Path path = FileSystems.getDefault().getPath("/path/file");
```

The following list defines some of the most important classes and interfaces of the API:

Files: This class consists exclusively of static methods that operate on files, directories, or other types of files.

Paths: This class consists exclusively of static methods that return a path by converting a path string or URI.

WatchService: An interface for watching various file-system events, such as create, delete, modify.

15.2 Reading Files

To read a text file, use BufferedReader.

```
1   public void readWithTry() {
2     Charset utf = StandardCharsets.UTF_8;
3     try (BufferReader reader = Files.newBufferedReader(path, utf)) {
4       for (String line = br.readLine(); line != null; line =
br.readLine())
5           System.out.println(line);
6       } catch (IOException e) {
7         e.printStackTrace();
8     }
9   }
```

The new *automatic resource management* feature of Java 7 makes dealing with resources, such as files, much easier. Before Java 7, users needed to explicitly close all open streams, causing some very verbose code. By using the preceding try statement, BufferedReader will be closed automatically.

However, in Groovy, this can be reduced to one line (leaving out exception handling), as follows:

```
1   println path.toFile().text
```

A getText() method is added to the File class in Groovy that simply reads the whole file.

15.3   Writing Files

Writing is similar to reading. For writing to text files, you should use PrintWriter. It includes the following methods (among others):

- print(Object): Prints the given object directly calling toString() on it

- println(Object): Prints the given object and then a newline

- println(): Prints the newline character sequence

- printf(String format, Object…args): Prints a formatted string using the given input

There are other ways to output to files, such as DataOutputStream, for example:

```
1   public void writeWithTry() {
2       try (FileOutputStream fos = new FileOutputStream("books.txt");
3                       DataOutputStream dos = new
                        DataOutputStream(fos)) {
4               dos.writeUTF("Modern Java");
5           } catch (IOException e) {
6               // log the exception
7           }
8   }
```

DataOutputStream allows an application to write primitive Java data types to an output stream. You can then use DataInputStream to read the data back in.

In Groovy, you can more easily write to a file, as follows:

```
1   new File("books.txt").text = "Modern Java"
```

Groovy adds a setText method to the File class, which allows this syntax to work.

15.4   Downloading Files

Although you might not ever do this in practice, its fairly simple to download a web page/file in code.

The following Java code opens an HTTP connection on the given URL (http://google.com, in this case), reads the data into a byte array, and prints out the resulting text.

```
1   URL url = new URL("http://google.com");
2   InputStream input = (InputStream) url.getContent();
3   ByteArrayOutputStream out = new ByteArrayOutputStream();
4   int n = 0;
5   byte[] arr = new  byte[1024];
6
7   while  (-1 != (n = input.read(arr)))
8       out.write(arr, 0, n);
9
10  System.out.println(new String(out.toByteArray()));
```

However, in Groovy, this also can be reduced to one line (leaving out exceptions).

```
1   println "http://google.com".toURL().text
```

A toURL() method is added to the String class, and a getText() method is added to the URL class in Groovy.

15.5   Summary

After reading this chapter, you should understand how to

- Explore the file system in Java

- Read from a file

- Write to a file

- Download the Internet

CHAPTER 16

Version Control

As soon as people start their programming careers, they are hit with the ton of bricks that is the version control system (VCS).

Version control software is used to keep track of, manage, and secure changes to files. This is a very important part of modern software development projects.

I am going to cover two popular ones, but there are many more:

- SVN (Subversion)
- Git (git)

Every VCS has the following basic actions:

- Add
- Commit
- Revert
- Remove
- Branch
- Merge

IDEs have plug-ins for dealing with version control systems and usually have built-in support for popular systems such as SVN and Git.

16.1   Subversion

SVN[1] was made as an improvement to an ancient and very popular VCS called CVS. It was a huge leap forward. Among other benefits, it allows any directory in the hierarchy to be checked out of the system and used.

---

[1] https://subversion.apache.org/.

© Adam L. Davis 2016
A. L. Davis, *Modern Programming Made Easy*, DOI 10.1007/978-1-4842-2490-8_16

To begin using SVN on the command line, you will check out a project and then commit files, as follows:

```
1   svn checkout http://example.com/svn/trunk
2   svn add file
3   svn commit
```

✎ Install SVN. Using your command prompt, check out a project from Google Code.[2] For example: svn checkout http://wiquery.googlecode.com/svn/trunk/ wiquery-read-only.

16.2   Git

Git[3] is a distributed version control system. This means that every copy of the source code contains the entire history of the code.

To begin using Git on a new project, simply run the following command:

```
1   git init
```

Create a file called README and then commit it, as follows:

```
1   git add README
2   git commit -m "this is my comment"
```

✎ Install Git. Go to github.com[4] and clone a repository. For example: git clone git@github.com:adamd/modern-java-examples.git.

16.3   Mercurial

Mercurial predates Git but is very similar to it. It's used for a lot of projects on Google Code and Bitbucket.[5]

✎ Install Mercurial. Go to Bitbucket and clone a repository using Mercurial. For example: hg clone https://bitbucket.org/adamldavis/dollar.

---

[2]http://googlecode.com.
[3]http://git-scm.com/.
[4]https://github.com/modernprog/part3.
[5]https://bitbucket.org/.

CHAPTER 17

The Interweb

(Courtesy xkcd: Interblag)

© Adam L. Davis 2016

A. L. Davis, *Modern Programming Made Easy*, DOI 10.1007/978-1-4842-2490-8_17

17.1   Web 101

The Web is a complex beast. Here's what you need to know:

- *Server*: The computer serving web pages

- *Client*: The computer that receives web pages and is used by a person

- *HTML*: The language used to create web pages

- *CSS*: "Cascading style-sheets"; store the styles of the web page

- *JavaScript*: A programming language that is used within web pages and executed on the client

17.2   My First Web App

You should make something very basic for your first web application. This way, you will have a better understanding of what's going on "behind the scenes" of many web frameworks.

Create a file called App.java and copy the following code into it:

```java
1   import java.io.IOException;
2   import java.io.OutputStream;
3   import java.net.InetSocketAddress;
4   import com.sun.net.httpserver.*;
5
6   public class App {
7
8       static class MyHandler implements HttpHandler {
9           public void handle(HttpExchange t) throws IOException {
10              String response = "<html> Hello Inter-webs! </html>";
11              t.sendResponseHeaders(200, response.length());
12              OutputStream os = t.getResponseBody();
13              os.write(response.getBytes());
14              os.close();
15          }
16      }
17
18      public static void main(String[] args) throws Exception {
19          HttpServer server = HttpServer.create(new InetSocketAddress(8000), 0);
20          server.createContext("/", new MyHandler());
21          server.setExecutor(null); // creates a default executor
22          server.start();
23          System.out.println("Server running at http://localhost:8000/");
24      }
25
26  }
```

All this does is create an `HttpServer` that listens for connections on port 8000 and responds with a message.

After running this code (`javac App.java && java App`), open your web browser and point it to `http://localhost:8000/`.

 `localhost` refers to the computer you're on, and `:8000` refers to port 8000.

Congratulations! You just made a web application!

It's not on the Internet yet, and it's extremely simple, but it's a good start.

PORT?

- *URL (Universal Resource Locator)*: The unique name used to locate resources on any network or machine. Sometimes it starts with "http"; sometimes it includes a port.

- *HTTP Hypertext Transfer Protocol*: The typical protocol used to communicate over the wire

- *Port*: A number that must be specified when communicating between computers (the default port for HTTP is 80)

17.3   The Holy Grails

Grails is a web framework for Groovy that follows the example of Ruby on Rails (hence *Grails*). It is an opinionated web framework with a command-line tool that gets things done really fast. Grails uses convention over configuration to reduce configuration overhead.

Grails lives firmly in the Java ecosystem and is built on technologies such as Spring and Hibernate. Grails also includes an object-relational mapping (ORM) framework called *GORM* and has a large collection of plug-ins.

17.3.1   Quick Overview

After installing Grails,[1] you can create an app by running the following on the command line:

```
1   $ grails create-app
```

---

[1]This overview is based on Grails 2.1.4, but the basics should remain the same for all versions of Grails.

Then, you can run commands such as `create-domain-class` and `generate-all` to create your application as you go. Run `grails help` to see the full list of commands available.

Grails applications have a very specific project structure. The following is a simple breakdown of *most* of that structure:

- `grails-app:` The Grails-specific folder

    - conf: Configuration, such as the data source and Bootstrap

    - controllers: Controllers with methods for index/create/edit/ delete, or anything else

    - domain: Domain model; classes representing your persistent data

    - i18n: Message bundles

    - jobs: Any scheduled jobs you might have go here

    - services: Back-end services in which your back end or "business" logic goes

    - taglib: You can very easily define your own tags for use in your GSP files.

    - views: Views of MVC; typically, these are GSP files (HTML-based)

- `src:` Any utilities or common code that doesn't fit anywhere else

    - java: Java code

    - groovy: Groovy code

- `web-app`

    - css: CSS style sheets

    - images: Images used by your web application

    - js: Your JavaScript files

    - WEB-INF: Spring's `applicationContext.xml` goes here.

To create a new domain (model) class, run the following:

```
1   $ grails create-domain-class
```

It's a good idea to include a package for your domain classes (such as `example.Post`).

A domain class in Grails also defines its mapping to the database. For example, here's a domain class representing a blogpost (assuming User and Comment have already been created):

```
1   class Post {
2       String text
3       int rating
4       Date created = new Date()
5       User createdBy
6
7       static hasMany = [comments: Comment]
8
9       static constraints = {
10          text(size:10..500)
11      }
12  }
```

The static hasMany field is a map that represents one-to-many relationships in your database. Grails uses Hibernate in the background to create tables for all your domain classes and relationships. Every table gets an id field for the primary key by default.

To have Grails automatically create your controller and views, run the following:

```
1   $ grails generate-all
```

⚠ Grails will ask if you want to overwrite existing files, if they exist. So, be careful when using this command.

When you want to test your app, you simply run the following:

```
1   $ grails run-app
```

When you're ready to deploy to a server, you can create a "war" file by typing this:

```
1   $ grails war
```

17.3.2   Plug-ins

The Grails ecosystem now includes over 1,000 plug-ins. To list all of the plug-ins, simply execute

```
1   $ grails list-plugins
```

When you've picked out a plug-in you want to use, execute the following (with the plug-in name and version):

```
1   $ grails install-plugin [NAME] [VERSION]
```

This will add the plug-in to your project. If you decide to uninstall it, simply use the `uninstall-plugin` command.

ⓘ **Only an Overview**   This has been only a brief overview of Grails. Many books have been written about Grails and how to use it. For more information on using Grails, please visit `grails.org`.[2]

17.4   Cloud

Grails is supported by the following cloud providers:

- CloudFoundry[3]
- Amazon[4]
- Heroku[5]

However, it is not within the scope of this book to go over all of them, so I'll talk talk about *Heroku*.

Heroku[6] is owned by Salesforce.com.[7] It was one of the first cloud platforms and has been in development since June 2007. When it began, it supported only Ruby, but it has since added support for Java, Scala, Groovy, Node.js, Clojure, and Python. Heroku supports multiple tiered accounts, including a free account.

Heroku relies on `git` for pushing changes to your server. For example, to create an app in Heroku using the CLI, do the following:

```
1    $ heroku create
2    $ git push heroku master
```

Your app will be up and running, and Heroku will identify the URL where you will find it.

 Go launch a Grails app on Heroku!

---

[2] `http://grails.org/`.
[3] `www.cloudfoundry.com/`.
[4] `http://aws.amazon.com/ec2/`.
[5] `www.heroku.com/`.
[6] `www.heroku.com/`.
[7] `http://news.heroku.com/news_releases/`
`salesforcecom-signs-definitive-agreement-to-acquire-heroku`.

17.5   The REST

REST stands for REpresentational State Transfer.[8] It was designed in a Ph.D. dissertation and has gained some popularity as the new web-service standard. Many developers have praised it as a much better standard than SOAP (which I will not attempt to describe).

At the most basic level in REST, each *CRUD* (create, read, update, delete) operation is mapped to an HTTP method.

- Create: POST

- Read: GET

- Update: PUT

- Delete: DELETE

The transport mechanism is assumed to be HTTP, but the message contents can be of any type, usually XML or JSON.

The JSR community has designed the JAX-RS API for building RESTful Java web services, while Groovy and Scala both have some built-in support for XML and JSON and various way of building web services.

17.5.1   Using Maven Archetypes

You can create a simple Java REST (JAX-RS) application using Maven, as follows:

```
1   mvn archetype:generate
```

Wait for things to download and then choose "tomcat-maven-archetype" (type "tomcat-maven" and press Enter, then type "1"; Enter; Enter). You will need to enter a groupId and artifactId.

After creating your application, you can start it by typing the following command:

```
1   mvn tomcat:run
```

17.6   Summary

Congratulations! You now understand the Interweb. Yes, it *is* a series of tubes. Ted Stevens (see following) was right!

> *...They want to deliver vast amounts of information over the Internet. And again, the Internet is not something that you just dump something on. It's not a big truck. It's a series of tubes. And if you don't understand, those tubes can be filled and if they are filled, when you put your message in, it gets in line and it's going to be delayed by anyone that puts into that tube enormous amounts of material, enormous amounts of material.*

> —Theodore "Ted" Fulton Stevens, Sr.—US senator from Alaska from December 24, 1968–January 3, 2009

---

[8]www.ics.uci.edu/~fielding/pubs/dissertation/top.htm.

■ ■ ■

CHAPTER 18

Swinging Graphics

Swing is the Java API for building cross-platform GUIs (graphical user interfaces).

If you ever want to write a graphical program (a computer game, for example), you will have to use Swing or some similar API.

There are many other libraries for doing graphics in Java, but Swing is built in.

 All of the code for this chapter can be found on the GitHub repository.[1]

18.1 Hello Window

The most basic concept of graphics is getting stuff onto the screen.

The easiest way to do this in Swing is to use JWindow, for example:

```java
import javax.swing.*;

public class HelloWindow extends JWindow {

    public HelloWindow() {
        setSize(500, 500); //width, height
        setAlwaysOnTop(true);
        setVisible(true);
    }

    @Override
    public void paint(Graphics g) {
        g.setFont(g.getFont().deriveFont(20f));
        g.drawString("Hello Window", 10, 20); //x,y
    }

```

[1]https://github.com/modernprog/part3.

© Adam L. Davis 2016
A. L. Davis, *Modern Programming Made Easy*, DOI 10.1007/978-1-4842-2490-8_18

```
17          public static void main(String[] args) {
18                  new HelloWindow();
19          }
20
21  }
```

Running this code will create a window at the top left of your screen, with the words "Hello Window" printed on it.

In the constructor, the following occurs:

- The width and height of the window are both set to 500 pixels.

- The window is set to always be displayed (above all other windows) with the setAlwaysOnTop method.

- Finally, setVisible(true) is called to make the window visible.

The paint method gets called every time the window is drawn on the screen. This method simply does the following:

- Sets the font size to 20

- Draws the string "Hello World" at coordinates x=10, y=20 (coordinates are always in pixels)

You might notice that the "window" doesn't have any edges, header, menu, or minimize/maximize icons that you're used to. To get these things, you use a JFrame. Here's a very simple example:

```
1   import javax.swing.*;
2
3   public class HelloFrame extends JFrame {
4
5           public HelloFrame() {
6                   super("Hello");
7                   setSize(500, 500);
8                   setAlwaysOnTop(true);
9                   setVisible(true);
10                  setDefaultCloseOperation(EXIT_ON_CLOSE);
11          }
12
13          public static void main(String[] args) {
14                  new HelloFrame();
15          }
16
17  }
```

Running this code creates a 500×500 "window with frame" with the name "Hello," and closing the window would exit the application.

18.2 Push My Buttons

Buttons are one of the ways that users can interact with your program. To cause something to happen when a button is pressed, you use an "ActionListener," for example:

```
1   JButton button = new  JButton("Talk!");
2   button.addActionListener(new  ActionListener() {
3       public void actionPerformed(ActionEvent e) {
4               JOptionPane.showMessageDialog(HelloFrame.this, "Hello!");
5       }
6   });
7   getContentPane().add(button);
```

Q The showMessageDialog method of JOptionPane is similar to JavaScript's alert method, in that it shows a pop-up window.

In Java 8, the ActionListener part can be shortened to the following:

```
1   button.addActionListener(e -> JOptionPane.showMessageDialog(this, "Hello!"));
```

The Groovy syntax is slightly different (it only requires a { and }).

```
1   button.addActionListener({e ->JOptionPane.showMessageDialog(this, "Hello!")})
```

Swing has many interfaces that end with the word "Listener," such as:

- KeyListener
- MouseListener
- WindowListener

The *Listener* pattern is very similar to the *Observer* design pattern.

18.3 Fake Browser

Let's make a web browser!
Let's begin by creating the fields and constructor for the class, as follows:

```
1   public class Browser extends JFrame {
2
3           JTextField urlField = new JTextField();
4           JEditorPane viewer = new JEditorPane();
5           JScrollPane pane = new JScrollPane();
6
```

```
7          public Browser() {
8                  super("Browser");
9                  setSize(800,600);
10                 setAlwaysOnTop(true);
11                 setDefaultCloseOperation(EXIT_ON_CLOSE);
12                 init();
13         }
```

JTextField will be used to input the URL. JEditorPane is used to show the HTML, and the JScrollPane allows the page to be scrollable.

Next, we define the init() method to put everything together.

```
1   private void init() {
2           viewer.setContentType("text/html");
3           pane.setViewportView(viewer);
4           JPanel panel = new JPanel();
5           panel.setLayout(new BorderLayout(2,2));
6           panel.add(pane, BorderLayout.CENTER);
7           panel.add(urlField, BorderLayout.NORTH);
8           getContentPane().add(panel);
9           urlField.addKeyListener(new KeyAdapter() {
10                  @Override
11                  public void keyReleased(KeyEvent e) {
12                          handleKeyPress(e);
13                  }
14          });
15  }
```

The viewer is set as the viewport view of the JScrollPane, so it can be scrolled.

JPanel is created with a BorderLayout. This allows us to arrange urlField on top of the scroll pane, much as in a real browser. KeyListener is used to call handleKeyPress whenever a key is pressed inside urlField.

Next, we fill out the handleKeyPress method.

```
1   private void handleKeyPress(KeyEvent e) {
2           if (e.getKeyCode() == KeyEvent.VK_ENTER) {
3                   try {
4                           viewer.setPage(new URL(urlField.getText()));
5                   } catch (MalformedURLException ex) {
6                           ex.printStackTrace();
7                   } catch (IOException ex) {
8                           ex.printStackTrace();
9                   }
10          }
11  }
```

This method simply sets the page of JEditorPane to the URL from urlField whenever the Enter key is pressed.

Finally, we define the main method.

```
1  public static void main(String[] args) {
2    new Browser().setVisible(true);
3  }
```

✎ **Eat your own dog food**   Run your app from Chapter 18. Open your fake browser, and point it to the app at http://localhost:8000/.

18.4   Griffon

Griffon[2] is a Groovy-based framework for creating Swing GUIs. It has a command-line interface very similar to Grails.

To begin a new project type, use the following:

```
1  griffon create-app griffon-example -archetype=jumpstart
```

Here, the name of the project is "griffon-example."

Griffon uses the MVC design pattern and Groovy DSL to make it much easier to build Swing applications.

18.5   Advanced Graphics

Although far beyond the scope of this book, there are several libraries that can be used for 2D or 3D graphics. Here are some of them.

Java 2D

- JavaFX[3]
- JFreeChart[4]
- Piccolo2D[5]
- JMagick[6]

---

[2]http://griffon.codehaus.org/
[3]www.oracle.com/technetwork/java/javafx/index.html
[4]www.jfree.org/jfreechart/
[5]www.piccolo2d.org/
[6]http://sourceforge.net/projects/jmagick/

Java 3D

- JOGL[7]

- JMonkeyEngine[8]

JavaScript 2D

- d3[9]

- Highcharts[10]

JavaScript 3D

- three.js[11]

18.6   Graphics Glossary

Component: Any graphical element defined in the Java graphics API

Double-Buffering: A technique used in graphics in which elements are drawn in memory before being sent to the computer screen. This avoids flicker.

Frame: In Swing, the frame (JFrame) is used to represent what we typically call a "window" in the GUI.

GUI: Graphical user interface

Layout: Strategy used by Swing for arranging components within a panel or other component

Menu: There are two kinds of menus: a windows built-in menu (JMenu) and a pop-up menu (JPopupMenu).

Menu item: In Swing, the JMenuItem represents one line of a menu that can have an action associated with it.

Panel: In Swing, JPanel is used to contain other components.

Pixel: Smallest unit of the screen that is drawable. A typical screen has millions of pixels that are arranged in a grid.

Window: Rectangular section of the screen. In Swing, the Window object has no border, so it can be used for a splash image, for example.

---

[7] http://download.java.net/media/jogl/www/.
[8] http://jmonkeyengine.org/.
[9] http://d3js.org/.
[10] www.highcharts.com/.
[11] http://threejs.org/.

18.7   Summary

You just learned the following:

- Creating a cross-platform GUI interface in Java and Groovy

- How to make a web browser worse than IE

- Some of the available graphics libraries

CHAPTER 19

Creating a Magical User Experience

First, you should be aware of the following acronyms:

UX: User experience

UI: User interface

KISS: Keep it simple, stupid

19.1   Application Hierarchy

You should prioritize your UX according to the following characteristics, from highest to lowest:

1. Functionality: Software does what it should.

2. Usefulness: Is the software easy to use?

3. Efficiency: Can the user work efficiently?

4. Magicalness: Is the experience magical?

You can't focus on being usable if your software is not functional. You can't focus on being efficient if your software is not usable.

After you have mastered all the basics (functionality, usability, and efficiency), only then can you attempt to make your UI magical.

19.2   Consider Your Audience

It's always important to consider the audience for your software. You should get to know them.

© Adam L. Davis 2016
A. L. Davis, *Modern Programming Made Easy*, DOI 10.1007/978-1-4842-2490-8_19

Those of you familiar with Harry Potter (or magic, in general) will recognize the words *wizard/witch* and *muggle*. In Potter's world, a *Squib* is someone who's aware of magic but not able to practice it, and a muggle is a normal person who's unware of magic.

We can apply this analogy to software.

- *Random User*: Muggle

- *Rock Star*: Squib

- *Genius*: Wizard/witch

19.3 Choice Is an Illusion

The more choices a person has, the more thinking they are required to do. As a designer, you should do the following:

- Limit choices

- Prepare for every possible choice

- Tailor choices for your audience

You will often have to decide whether to give your user a choice or make the choice for them.

The easy way is always to let the user decide, but the better way is generally to give the user one less choice. This will make your software simpler and, therefore, easier to use.

19.4 Direction

Work instinctively—instinct is your friend. Motion is a subtle and effective way of getting the user's attention. Of course, too much motion is a distraction, so it should be kept to a minimum.

Another instinctual image is the human face. Faces are noticed first. This is why you always see faces on the left-hand side of text (in languages that read from left to right). The eye is drawn first to the face and then to the accompanying text.

19.5 Skuemorphism

Skuemorph: is something from real life that is imitated in software.

Simulating real-life features, such as edges, bevels, and buttons, can be useful for communicating *affordability* (what the user can do with something). However, you have to get it 100% right, if you're simulating a complete object (such as a book). This is why skuemorphism is generally a bad idea. Imitating something from the real world comes across as fake, if it is not done perfectly.

Windows 8 exemplifies the opposite approach—it attempts to remove all metaphor. The new UI of Windows (sometimes called Metro) is very flat and edgeless. Of course, you can take this concept too far. For example, what is clickable should still be obvious.

19.6   Context Is Important

Three stars with no context could mean anything. However, given context (3/5 stars), what is meant becomes obvious.

Also, context is important for navigation. It must be obvious where the user is in your software at all times and how to navigate somewhere else. Otherwise, your users will feel lost, which is not a comfortable feeling.

A related concept is to avoid "modes." The more ways there are to interact with the software, the more complex it will seem.

19.7   KISS

Above all, keep things simple—simple for the user. For example, in general, there should always be one way to do something in the software. Also, as a general rule, your UI should follow the conventions set by existing software/web sites (for example, always underline links).

As your software grows, you will constantly have to make choices about new UI features. In addition to other considerations, you should also contemplate how they can be made simpler.

19.8   You Are Not the User

Unless you are building software only for yourself, the overwhelming probability is that your users are very different from you. For this reason, you must not only try to think like your user but also really get to know him or her.

This means ideally that you sit down and watch your users operate the software.

19.9   Summary

From this chapter, you should have learned the following:

- Your UI should be functional, usable, and efficient, in that order.

- Consider who your user is during all phases of design

- Limit choices and handle all conditions

- Instinct is your friend, but don't imitate reality.

- Keep things simple for users and listen to them

For more about usability, I highly recommend Steve Krug's *Don't Make Me Think* (New Riders, 2014).

CHAPTER 20

Databases

Databases are an extremely important component of most software projects.

If you're not familiar with a database, it is a software system that stores data and enables calculations on those data, somewhat like a spreadsheet.

An original database is known as a *relational database*, because it stores relationships between tables in the database. A database typically consists of several highly structured data tables with defined constraints. For example, each column of a table has a type, whether or not it can be null, if it must be unique, and other constraints.

There is a highly standardized language for performing operations and calculations on a database called *SQL* (Structured Query Language). SQL has been around a long time and could easily warrant its own book, so I will only cover the basics here.

Since the advent of so-called big-data projects (such as a particular "face"-themed social network), a second category of databases has emerged: NoSQL databases. Typically, these are more like key-value pairs than relational databases. They include Redis, MongoDB, Cassandra, and many others.

Note The SQL/NoSQL categorization is an oversimplification, but it provides an easier narrative than the actual complex reality. In other words, "Here be dragons!"

20.1 SQL (Relational) Databases

Part of classic relational databases is the concept of ACID[1] (atomicity, consistency, isolation, durability). To summarize ACID, it means that the database is always in a consistent state (with enforced constraints), even if the system crashes in the middle of an update. For example, if a column in a table is marked as "non null," it will never be null. This may seem like a simple thing to achieve, but it is actually very hard.

 Some good open source databases include PostgreSQL, MySQL, and H2.

---

[1]`https://en.wikipedia.org/wiki/ACID`.

© Adam L. Davis 2016
A. L. Davis, *Modern Programming Made Easy*, DOI 10.1007/978-1-4842-2490-8_20

20.1.1   SQL

The basic language of relational databases is SQL. It includes the ability to define tables and perform complex queries on those tables.

For example, creating a table looks something like the following:

```
1   CREATE TABLE dragon(
2       dragon_id INTEGER,
3       dragon_name VARCHAR(100),
4       birth_date DATE NOT NULL,
5       PRIMARY KEY (dragon_id)
6   );
```

A table always needs to have a primary key—it acts as the identifier for each row of the table. In this case, the primary key is dragon_id.

Database types cover the basics, such as INTEGER, but other unfamiliar types include the following:

- VARCHAR(length) is similar to the String object. It has a given maximum length.

- TIMESTAMP is used to store dates and times.

- NUMERIC(precision, scale) or DECIMAL(precision, scale) is used to store numbers such as currency values (for example, the number 123.45 has a precision of 5 and a scale of 2).

- BLOB is typically used to store binary data.

To find the birthday of your oldest dragon, you might perform the following query:

```
1   SELECT MIN(birth_date) FROM dragon;
```

Or, to select all dragons whose names start with *S* (in alphabetic order), run the following:

```
1   SELECT dragon_id, dragon_name FROM dragon
2       WHERE dragon_name LIKE 'S%'
3       ORDER BY dragon_name;
```

20.1.2   Foreign Keys

A *foreign key* is simply a column in a table that references the primary key of another table.

For example, let's say you have a wizard table, and each wizard has multiple dragons they keep as pets. If the wizard table's primary key is wizard_id, the "dragon" table would have the following column and foreign key constraint:

```
1   owner INTEGER,
2   FOREIGN KEY owner REFERENCES wizard (wizard_id)
```

Although SQL keywords are shown in uppercase, this is not required by all databases.

20.1.3 Connections

A database system typically runs as a separate process, and your code connects to it in some way.

There are many different ways to do this.

In Java, the most basic standard for connecting to databases is called JDBC.

It allows you to run SQL statements on the database. You will need a specific *driver* for your database.

There are also *object-relational mapping* (ORM) frameworks, such as Hibernate.[2] These frameworks have you map Java objects to data tables. They are built *on top of* JDBC. For example, Hibernate has its own query language, called HQL, which is translated into SQL by Hibernate. Grails uses Hibernate.

Alternatively, there are code-generating frameworks that allow you to use a DSL for queries. One such framework for Java is jOOQ.[3] It allows you to write type-safe queries in the native language. For example:

```
1  create.selectFrom(DRAGON)
2    .where(DRAGON.NAME.like("S%"))
3    .orderBy(DRAGON.NAME)
```

20.2 NoSQL Databases

Big web projects (such as Wikipedia) had problems using relational databases to scale up to millions of users. They had to partition their database onto multiple machines (called *sharding*), which broke foreign key references. So, over time, big-data projects moved to NoSQL databases, which are basically key-value stores that can be scaled up more easily.

NoSQL databases are used by Netflix, Reddit, Twitter, GitHub, Pinterest, eBay, eHarmony, craigslist, and many others.

▓ **Note**   I will cover some NoSQL databases here, but there are many others.

---

[2]http://hibernate.org/orm/.
[3]http://jooq.org/.

20.2.1   Redis

Redis[4] is a key-value store. Everything is stored as a string in Redis, including binary data. It's written in C and has a long list of commands.[5]

There are multiple clients for using Redis from many different languages, including Java, Node.js, Scala, Ruby, Python, and Go.

20.2.2   MongoDB

MongoDB[6] calls itself a document database. It stores JSON-style (JavaScript) documents and has a rich query syntax. It's written in C++, but JavaScript can be used in queries and aggregation functions.

MongoDB supports indexing of any field in a document. It scales horizontally using sharding and provides high availability and increased throughput using replication.

MongoDB can also be used as a file system.

20.2.3   Cassandra

Cassandra[7] was originally developed at Facebook and was released as an open source project in July 2008. It's written in Java and is now a mature, top-level Apache project.

Cassandra is scalable, decentralized, fault-tolerant, and has tunable consistency. It also uses replication for fault-tolerance and performance.

Cassandra has an SQL-like alternative called *CQL* (Cassandra Query Language). Language drivers are available for Java (JDBC), Python (DBAPI2), and Node.JS (Helenus).

20.2.4   VoltDB

VoltDB[8] provides a counter-example to the SQL/NoSQL divide. It's distributed, in-memory, and lightning-fast, but it's also a relational database and supports SQL.

20.3   Summary

- There are two major types of databases: SQL and NoSQL.

- Relational (SQL) databases are highly structured, consistent, and durable, but difficult to scale up.

- Big-data projects tend to use NoSQL databases, which are key-value stores that can be scaled up more easily.

---

[4] http://redis.io/.
[5] http://redis.io/commands.
[6] www.mongodb.org/.
[7] http://cassandra.apache.org/.
[8] http://voltdb.com/.

CHAPTER 21

Conclusion

If you've gotten this far, congratulations! You probably know a lot more than when you started (I hope). This book ended up being a lot longer than I initially planned, and, at first, some readers might even have thought, "Hey! That's not easy!"

It turns out that programming can be challenging and complex. There are many layers to a typical program covering different levels of abstraction, and a whole version-control mess, if you work on a large team. However, I stand by the title of the book. To me, what really makes something easy is if it's fun or rewarding. If it's not fun or rewarding, even the simplest task, such as doing dishes, seems difficult. However, if something is fun, a person will be inclined to spend hours a day at it, becoming a master through practice over time.

I hope that you have found something fun in this book. If not, please think of an alternative you do find fun or rewarding (sports, music, movies, whatever) and write a program related to it. That is the best way to learn programming.

© Adam L. Davis 2016   111
A. L. Davis, *Modern Programming Made Easy*, DOI 10.1007/978-1-4842-2490-8_21

Appendixes

Appendix A: Java/Groovy[1]

Feature	Java	Groovy
Public class	public class	class
Loops	for(Type it : c){...}	c.each {...}
Lists	List list = asList(1,2,3);	def list = [1,2,3]
Maps	Map m = ...; m.put(x,y);	def m = [x: y]
Function def.	void method(Type t) {}	def method(t) {}
Mutable value	Type t	def t
Immutable value	final Type t	final t
Null safety	(x == null ? null : x.y)	x?.y
Null replacement	(x == null ? "y" : x)	x ?: "y"
Sort	Collections.sort(list)	list.sort()
Wildcard import	import java.util.*;	import java.util.*
Var-args	(String... args)	(String... args)
Type parameters	Class<T>	Class<T>
Concurrency	Fork/Join	GPars

---

[1]Version 1.3 of this cheat sheet.

© Adam L. Davis 2016
A. L. Davis, *Modern Programming Made Easy*, DOI 10.1007/978-1-4842-2490-8

No Java Analog

Feature	Groovy
Default closure arg.	`it`
Default value	`def method(t = "yes")`
Add method to object	`t.metaClass.method  =  {}`
Auto-delegate	`@Delegate`
Extension methods	`Categories`
Rename import	`import java.util.Vector as Vect`

Tricks

Feature	Groovy
Range	`def range = [a..z]`
Slice	`def slice = list[0..3]`
<< Operator	`list << addMeToList`
Cast operation	`def dog = [name: "Fido", speak:{println "woof"}] as Dog`
GString	`def gString = "Dog's name is ${dog.name}"`

Appendix B: Java/Scala[2]

Feature	Java	Scala
Public Class	public class	class
Loops	for(Type it : c){...}	c.foreach {...}
Lists	List list = asList(1,2,3);	val list = List(1,2,3)
Maps	Map m = ...; m.put(x,y);	val m = Map(x -> y)
Function Def.	void method(Type t) {}	def method(t: Type) = {}
Mutable Value	Type t	var t: Type
Immutable Value	final Type t	val t: Type
Null safety	(x == null ? null : x.y)	for (a <- Option(x)) yield a.y
Null replacement	(x == null ? "y" : x)	Option(x) getOrElse "y"
Sort	Collections.sort(list)	list.sort(_ < _)
Wildcard import	import java.util.*;	import scala.collection._
Var-args	(String... args)	(args: String*)
Type parameters	Class<T>	Class[T]
Concurrency	Fork/Join	Akka

No Java Analog

Feature	Scala
Default closure arg.	_ (underscore is positionally matched)
Default value	def method(t:String = "yes")
Add method to object	use Trait
Auto-delegate	use Trait
Extension methods	implicit class
Rename import	import scala.collection.{Vector => Vect}

---

[2]Version 1.3 of this cheat sheet.

115

Null, Nil, Etc.

Type	Description
Null	A Trait with one instance, null, similar to Java's null.
Nil	Represents an empty List of zero length.
Nothing	A Trait that is a subtype of everything. There are no instances of it.
None	None signifies no result. Option has two subclasses: Some and None.
Unit	Type to use on a method that does not return a value

Appendix C: Java/JavaScript[3]

Feature	Java	JavaScript
Public class	public class	function
Loops	for(Type it : c){...}	c.forEach(function(){...})
Lists	List list = asList(1,2,3);	var list = [1,2,3]
Maps	Map m = ...; m.put(x,y);	var m = {x: y}
Function def.	void method(Type t) {}	function method(t) {}
Mutable value	Type t	var t
Immutable value	final Type t	const t
Null safety	(x == null ? null : x.y)	(x == null ? null : x.y)
Null replacement	(x == null ? "y" : x)	x ? x : 'y'
Sort	Collections.sort(list)	list.sort()
Wildcard import	import java.util.*;	N/A
Var-args	(String... args)	()
Type parameters	Class<T>	N/A
Concurrency	Fork/Join	

No Java Analogue

Feature	JavaScript
Add method to object	t.method = function() {}
Extension methods	Type.prototype.method = function() {}

---

[3]Version 1.2 of this cheat sheet.

Appendix D: Resources

- Java Tutorials[4]
- Java Docs[5]
- Groovy Docs[6]
- Scala Docs[7]
- Grails Docs[8]
- Play Docs[9]
- Heroku Dev Center[10]
- JavaOne (by going to Tools ➤ Content Catalog[11])
- StackOverflow[12]
- Free Programming Books[13]

---

[4]http://docs.oracle.com/javase/tutorial/.
[5]http://docs.oracle.com/javase/7/docs/api/.
[6]http://groovy.codehaus.org/Documentation.
[7]www.scala-lang.org/documentation/.
[8]http://grails.org/learn.
[9]www.playframework.com/documentation/2.2.x/Home.
[10]https://devcenter.heroku.com/.
[11]www.oracle.com/javaone/index.html.
[12]http://stackoverflow.com/.
[13]https://github.com/vhf/free-programming-books/blob/master/free-programming-books.md.

Appendix E: Free Online Learning

Khan Academy[14] is amazing. If you haven't seen it yet, please take a look. The founder started out by teaching his cousins remotely and putting the videos on YouTube. He then created hundreds of videos, teaching millions of people. Khan Academy encompasses nearly every subject: science, math, finance, history, computer science, and more. The amazing thing is, it's all free!

Contrast this, for example, with the price of higher education in the United States. It's been skyrocketing,[15] owing partly to government-funded student loans and partly to other factors.

Online education is flourishing. Many classes in this space are free or very inexpensive. Coursera[16] allows students to take courses from leading institutions, such as Stanford, Princeton, and Emory University. Online interactive platforms such as Codecademy[17] (free) and Codeschool[18] (selectively free) offer to teach you to program.

The Death of College?

Is there any point in going to college anymore? College offers so many benefits other than the obvious textbook knowledge: learning to work with others, the social life, athletics, and accountability (not to mention the prestige associated with a degree). However, it seems like these benefits could be achieved in different, less expensive ways—perhaps not a degree but something like certificates, which could be just as useful.

You've probably been able to simply buy books and teach yourself, or learn by doing, so let's not overestimate the potential of online learning. However, with so many alternatives cropping up, and the advantages of college being questionable, it's easy to imagine education being less expensive in the future.

Money

Sure that's all great, but are these "schools" sustainable? What is the business model? Well, Khan Academy is a not-for-profit[19] venture, so its future is entirely dependent on the generosity of donors. The other institutions cited are conventional companies. Some offer free samplers, with normal courses requiring tuition.

Coursera and its peers will most likely charge only for the certificate,[20] not the actual learning. This is a promising business model.

---

[14]www.khanacademy.org/.
[15]https://en.wikipedia.org/wiki/Higher_Education_Price_Index.
[16]www.coursera.org.
[17]www.codecademy.com/learn.
[18]www.codeschool.com/.
[19]www.khanacademy.org/about.
[20]www.quora.com/Coursera/What-is-Courseras-business-model/answer/Franck-Dernoncourt.

More Online Resources

The following is a list of various web sites offering the opportunity to learn just about anything:

- *Khan Academy*[21]: Math, Python

- *Codecademy*[22]: JavaScript, HTML/CSS, PHP, Python, Ruby

- *Coursera*[23]: Algorithms, Programming, etc.

- *Codeschool*[24]: Ruby, JavaScript, HTML/CSS, iOS

- *Udacity*[25]: Everything from "Introduction to Computer Science" to "Applied Cryptography"

- *CodeCombat*[26]: Learn JavaScript through a game

---

[21]www.khanacademy.org/.
[22]www.codecademy.com/learn.
[23]www.coursera.org/courses.
[24]www.codeschool.com/.
[25]www.udacity.com/.
[26]http://codecombat.com/.

Appendix F: Java

Java[27] was first developed in the 90s by James Gosling. It borrowed much of its syntax from C and C++, to be more appealing to programmers at the time. Java was owned by Sun Microsystems, which was acquired by Oracle in 2010.

Java is a *statically typed, object-oriented* language. "Statically typed" means that every variable and parameter must have a defined type, as opposed to languages such as JavaScript, which are dynamically typed. "Object-oriented" (OO) means that data and functions are grouped into objects (functions are usually referred to as *methods* in OO languages).

Java code is compiled to bytecode that runs on a virtual machine (the Java Virtual Machine, JVM). The virtual machine handles garbage collection and allows Java to be compiled once and run on any OS or hardware that has a JVM. This is an advantage over C/C++, which must be compiled directly to machine code and has no automatic garbage collection (the programmer has to allocate and de-allocate memory).

The standard implementation of the JVM is packaged in two different ways: the JRE (Java Runtime Environment) and the JDK (Java Development Kit). The JRE is strictly for running Java as an end user, while the JDK is for developing Java code. The JDK comes with the javac command for compiling Java code to bytecode, among other things.

As of this writing, Java is one of the most popular programming languages in use,[28] particularly for server-side web applications.

The Java ecosystem is huge. It's mainly composed of JVMs, libraries, tools, and IDEs. If you'd like to learn more, you could read Modern Java[29] which delves more deeply into the ecosystem.

---

[27] Java is a registered trademark of Oracle.
[28] www.tiobe.com/index.php/content/paperinfo/tpci/index.html.
[29] https://leanpub.com/modernjava.

Index

Get the eBook for only $4.99!

Why limit yourself?

Now you can take the weightless companion with you wherever you go and access your content on your PC, phone, tablet, or reader.

Since you've purchased this print book, we are happy to offer you the eBook for just $4.99.

Convenient and fully searchable, the PDF version enables you to easily find and copy code—or perform examples by quickly toggling between instructions and applications.

To learn more, go to http://www.apress.com/us/shop/companion or contact support@apress.com.

Apress®
THE EXPERT'S VOICE™

Printed in the United States
By Bookmasters